let's help
our
children
talk

First Published 1977
The O'Brien Press
11 Clare Street Dublin 2 Ireland

ISBN 0 905140 20 6 Bound
ISBN 0 905140 21 4 Paper

Illustrations by Pat Walsh
Cover Design Jarlath Hayes
Layout and Design Michael O'Brien

Printed by E. & T. O'Brien Ltd.
11 Clare Street Dublin 2 Ireland.

Binding John F. Newman
Typesetting Redsetter Limited

let's help our children talk

Miriam Gallagher

THE O'BRIEN PRESS
11 CLARE ST DUBLIN 2

Contents

Introduction

'How does a child learn to talk?' 'How can language be stimulated?' 'Should a child's speech be corrected?' 'What can I do if my child stammers?' 'Why doesn't he talk?'

The aim of this book is to answer some of these questions by illustrating the various stages in the learning of language and by highlighting some of the most common speech problems in young children. The book is intended as a general guide for parents, teachers and those in contact with young children. The parents of children attending speech therapy clinics, child guidance clinics, and parents whose children have special problems such as deafness, mental handicap, autism etc., will of course be guided specifically by those working with their children. I have included a list of useful addresses for any parents who do not know where to seek help.

The book is intended for the intelligent layman and where possible jargon has been omitted. I have used the term 'mother' to denote 'mother', 'father', 'parents' or group of adults involved in rearing the baby and young child. To avoid clumsiness and in view of the fact that more boys than girls suffer from speech difficulties, I have alluded to the child as 'him' all through the book. Some readers may not be familiar with all the words used and for them I have added a glossary of terms for easy reference. The views I express are my own. Written sources influencing my views are indicated in the references and bibliography. Living sources which influenced me include my own children and the children with whom I have worked.

I'd like to acknowledge the helpful comments of colleagues and friends and to thank the Director of the Dublin College of Speech Therapy for providing library facilities.

I am indebted to my children Mia, Donnchadha and Etain who provided samples of language and to my husband Gerhardt for his positive criticism and encouragement.

While out walking, talk about what you see.

Part One
How Children Learn To Talk

1
Birth To Twelve Months

Babbling
Learning to Hear
Guidelines at a Glance

1
Birth To Twelve Months

MAN RELATES TO his family, the community and its culture through the spoken word. Through language he expresses his thoughts and emotions. The child must learn to develop language to the best of his ability in order to survive in society. How can we help our children talk?

To help effectively it is important to know something of the growth of a child — the first five years of life crucially affect how he will develop intellectually and emotionally. During the first year of life he is establishing a tie with his mother and our civilization emphasises the importance of the mother-child relationship. Within the framework of this relationship and against the background of the child's environment, we can trace the milestones in his speech and language development. This will help to highlight some of his specific needs during these early years.

Let's take a look at the growth of the baby from birth to school age. It is important to realise that each child progresses at his own individual pace when considering the stages of development[1] which follow. The skills involved in the process of talking are being developed from the moment a baby is born and utters his first cry. His first

10

sounds arise from bodily discomfort. He cries lustily when hungry or uncomfortable. The sucking and swallowing movements he makes when feeding help him to prepare for the development of speech. When one part of his body is stimulated, the whole body becomes active. He is startled by sudden loud noises. He stiffens, blinks, quivers, screws up his eyes, extends his limbs and may cry. Reflex smiling movements occur in response to stimulation. If his face is stroked, he may 'smile'; he can lift his head occasionally and can push away an adult's finger when it is pressed against his chin.

The new baby spends the first month or so adjusting to his environment. At the end of the first month of life he can be calmed and can stop whimpering if he hears a soothing voice near him. Added to his crying and whimpering sounds, he sighs and makes throaty grunts. During his second month, he is able to follow a horizontally moving light with his eyes. He will laugh and begin to smile socially if an adult's voice is accompanied by smiling and eye contact. Many mothers can tell by this time whether a baby is crying for food or because he is 'windy'. He is beginning to get more muscular control and can turn his head from side to side — when he is three months old, he can sit with support. He is starting to associate his mother's voice with the pleasures of his life, cuddling, feeding, bathing and he is beginning to react to the voice itself and will smile when he hears it, cooing and chuckling with delight. At first all sounds are meaningless to him but he is starting to notice the tone of voice. One of the early discriminations that he learns to make is between a pleased and displeased tone of voice. He cries at the angry tone and smiles when the tone is friendly.

His cry of distress is one form of action, the way he vigorously seeks the breast or bottle is another, his squirming during feeding yet another. The baby needs to learn that the noises spoken by other people have a meaning and that by making similar noises he can influence what people do. He looks at the person who is talking to him and replies with his own cries, grunts and crowing sounds.

Even at this early stage, the baby needs to be talked to as this will help him to get on with the vital process of listening. The mother who talks to her baby while feeding, bathing and cuddling him, linking what is said with what interests the baby, is helping him to become aware that speech is connected in a special way with his world. The seeds are being sown for a ripe harvest of language when he becomes ready to talk. About the start of the fourth month of life, the baby can sit up easily with support and he will take and hold an object. When he hears a voice he turns his eyes and his head in the direction of the voice. About this time he enters a vitally important stage in his speech and language development, namely that of babbling.

BABBLING

The baby has begun to respond to speech by making noises himself, at first vocal glides which contain variation of pitch and volume. He can express his feelings through his voice. He uses a rising inflection if surprised or pleased and a falling inflection if disappointed. By now he is babbling repeating chains of syllables, ga-ga-ga-ga-, ba-ba-ba-ba-ba, ma-mamamamamamama. He is experiencing the feel and listening to the sound of his own voice. He will repeat a sound that intrigues him, crow with delight, and then set off on another vocal experiment. He is getting a great kick out of these vocal explorations which take place amid much laughing and smiling. When his mother reacts to his noises with a great smile of maternal pride, this can in turn stimulate the baby to increase his vocal play. Most babies babble freely after food and drink. The baby is constantly adding to his repertoire of sounds by self-imitation and he does this more frequently on his own. If an adult's voice interrupts him he either steps up his own babbling practice or stops altogether. Occasionally if the syllable being spoken is said gently by an adult, creating no interruption in the rhythm of the baby's flow of babbling, it can be reinforcing. About the fifth month, he responds automatically to a friendly voice by smiling and to an angry voice by crying. He shows his displeasure if a favourite toy is removed. About the sixth month he will reach for an object and get the taste and feel of it by putting it into his mouth. He can roll from his back onto his tummy and can sit alone for about thirty seconds. He is getting stronger and can grasp a dangling object and he can hold two cubes — he no longer reacts automatically to friendly or angry voices but rather to the facial expression accompanying the voice. He can follow a vertically moving object with his eyes. His babbling consists of not only a repetitive chain of syllables, guh-guh-guh-guh or, nja-nja-nja, but there is also a marked rhythm. He often starts in a whisper, rises to a crescendo and then subsides: m-ma-ma-Ma-Ma-Ma-Ma-MaMaMaMamamamama.

By the sixth month, the normal pattern of

intonation of phrases and vowel sounds can be recognised in sounds the baby makes. During the seventh month he can sit alone easily and may have cut his first teeth. He stretches out his arms to his mother, the first person with whom he is establishing a relationship. He usually rejects adults' demands for imitation but occasionally will form sounds with silent mouth movements. His babbling contains more variety. Sometimes he combines two vowel sounds ba-ga – or he can stick to the same sounds for several days, practising these at his own pace and for his own satisfaction.

Towards the end of the eighth month, the baby begins to alter his babbling, suddenly changing the pitch, repeating the commanding, complaining, declaring, questioning intonations of adults. He uses the 'mama', 'dada', 'bye bye' words so often spoken by his parents more as a form of babbling than as actual words.

If an adult imitates the baby's pounding or clapping, he will step up his own pounding and clapping. By the end of the eighth month, the baby will imitate the adult's physical rhythmic movements, nodding, clapping etc. as can be seen from the popular 'clap handies, clap handies till Dada comes home' sung or spoken by an adult with marked rhythm. By this time the baby is crawling and can stand with help. He will offer a toy to an adult. About the ninth month, he looks at a person or object named and he is starting to understand some words if gesture is used. He can, but doesn't always, stop crawling into the coal scuttle or messing the cat's food, if he hears 'no - no'. He will imitate sounds he hears in his own way. By this stage he can stand, holding onto furniture and is well able to sit up alone – he makes little stepping movements and sways to music. He holds out his arms to an adult who prepares to pick him up. He responds to strangers by crying or retreating and to other children by exploration or crying. His crying has more variety of pitches and he yells lustily to attract attention.

About the tenth month, he can understand some words, particularly his own name and those of his family. He has already begun to respond to adult stimulation, no longer automatically, but with more discrimination. He shakes his head for 'no' and waves 'bye-bye' on request. He will make great efforts to imitate syllables, particularly if an adult interrupts his babbling by saying the sound he is practising. If in the middle of saying BABABABABABABA, his mother says 'BABA', without disturbing the rhythmic flow, the baby is more likely at this stage to say 'Bah' or 'BABA' rather than unlike syllables such as 'wa' or 'gaga' which he would have said at an earlier stage.

When he is eleven months, he enjoys listening to music and voices. He uses the sounds m,b,d,h, ing, z,g,p,t,k. He will imitate sounds already practised and sometimes new ones.

By the time his first birthday arrives, he may be walking and have one or two words in his vocabulary; he pays great attention to individual words if they are always associated with things or activities which are important to his needs. Some of these words could be 'teddy', 'milk', 'bath', 'water', 'Mama', 'Dada'. He often responds by trying to imitate the words as best he can — 'wawa' for water, 'mih' for milk.

The rate at which a baby prepares to develop speech varies with each individual so there are no hard and fast rules. The baby progresses from crying, cooing, crowing and gurgling to babbling. When the babbling period is delayed or interrupted through illness, true speech can also be delayed. Deaf babies start to babble at the normal time but since they cannot hear their own sounds adequately, they tend to lose interest and consequently have far less vocal play than babies with normal hearing.

We can't accept the babbling, 'mama' or 'dada' made by the baby sometimes between his sixth and ninth month as the child's first words, since to say 'mama' or 'dada', without having anything in mind except the sounds themselves, is not talking. It is not until the second year of life that real talking begins. It is then that the baby reacts to sounds, closely associated with particular objects, situations and activities, as *meanings* and starts to use them as names. However we can find babies of average intelligence who use one or two words clearly and intelligently before their first birthday. During the first year of life, the baby has learnt to focus his eyes, smile and babble. He has learnt to discover and use his limbs. He has some of his teeth. His personality is emerging and he is getting to know the world while growing within the warmth and security of his family. During his first year, he is learning to hear, understand and to talk.

The connection between speaking and hearing is an obvious one but for this reason we mustn't take it that the connection is automatic. Both are vitally important for the child's speech and language development and are going on at the same time. So let's take a brief look now at what learning to hear really means.

Sounds which come from the world around us are received and transformed by our ears. We really hear with our brains. In order to do this, sounds must be carried there to be registered. The outer ear, which is shaped like a funnel, collects the sounds and transmits them to the middle ear where the vibrations of the ear drum are transmitted to the inner ear. Sounds arrive as pressure waves in the air and are changed in the ear into electrical waves, which are carried by nerve pathways to the brain. This, in simple terms is how we hear all the wonderful, terrifying and exciting sounds of our universe.

The baby starts learning to hear from the moment he is born. The miracle is that he should learn so much about sound in so short a time. At first his response to sound is a reflex one — he will jerk his body when he hears a loud noise long before he is able to lift his head and turn it towards the source of a sound, he will turn his eyes towards the sound. At two and a half months a loud noise doesn't startle him quite as much and as he grows older he begins to substitute a learned response for the earlier startle response. By eight and a half months of age, he turns and recognises the source of a sound. The sounds he hears most often become familiar and he has learnt that many sounds have a meaning: his mother's voice, the sound of his rattle, a cup being tapped with a spoon. He begins to reproduce the sounds around him and this reproduction is based on the preceding months of listening and learning to discriminate — the baby has been *learning to hear*.

Make sure your baby has plenty of opportunity to hear normal speech, familiar sounds and music.

Guidelines

BIRTH TO TWELVE MONTHS

Your child is learning to *talk*. Help him by saying a few vowel sounds as you smile at him, waiting the four or five seconds the baby needs before he responds.

Talk to your baby clearly and simply and in a normal tone of voice.

Use speech while you are doing the everyday things, feeding, washing, walking etc.

Your child is learning to *hear*. Let him listen to normal speech, familiar sounds, rhythm games and songs.

Show books to your baby, talking to him about the pictures.

Don't be upset by comparisons between your baby's speech and that of another.

Remember speech and language development are individual.

Contact your doctor or local health clinic if you *suspect* any hearing loss in your baby or if in doubt about his developmental progress.

2
Twelve To
Thirty-Six Months

First Words
Jargon
First Phrases
Essential Factors
Guidelines at a Glance

2

Twelve To Thirty-Six Months

TO THE ONE-YEAR-OLD, life is an exciting place. During his first twelve months he has been learning that his basic needs can be satisfied by his mother, that his world is orderly and predictable and that to be alive makes sense. He has been learning to hear and produce the sounds and syllables necessary for meaningful speech – during the next period, lasting about two years, he must learn to walk, talk and establish himself as a person separate from other people. He must also learn about self control and develop self-esteem. Let's take a look at his progress during this time.

FIRST WORDS

Sometime between the tenth and eighteenth month, the child usually learns to say his first true words. He shows great interest in isolated adult words and pays great attention when they are used in connection with objects and activities important to his needs – he will sometimes imitate sounds made by clocks, dogs, cows and adult exclamations – 'tick tock', 'bow wow', 'moo', 'oh good!', etc. At the age of twelve months he understands simple commands such as 'give me the spoon', 'say 'bye-'bye' — he is practising for future fluent speech by babbling long streams of tuneful sounds. He will use gesture, pointing to someone or something that interests him during this fluency practice. While he is being dressed, he holds out his foot for his shoe and an arm for a sleeve. He associates words with various objects and tries to say the word — e.g. 'mih' for milk, 'poon' for spoon. When he has acquired his first words, he starts to repeat them in order to reinforce them. He learns the names of things interesting to *him* and needs to hear the labels of many things many times before he will use these names in phrases. The first words of a child may sound very much like those of adult speech but they differ greatly in meaning. At first Dada may mean 'men' rather than 'father' — 'dolly' could mean any toy. 'Ball' could mean, 'I want the ball', 'throw me the ball' or 'get rid of that horrible ball'; 'doggy' may be used to cover all kinds of four-legged furry creatures. Only gradually do meanings approximate to those usual among adults.

By the time he is fifteen months he points to a picture when his mother names it. He acquires four or five new words and says the equivalent of 'thank you'; he likes to take off his shoes and is able to walk a few steps — some children of this age will of course be walking much more than a few steps! The independent but messy business of learning to feed himself has begun. He is able to lift the cup to his lips but apt to spill. He grasps the spoon and tries to put the food into his mouth. Allowing him opportunity to feed himself ensures that he learns to use whichever hand is natural for him and also helps him towards independence.

At first he'll probably hurl his food across the

room, sweetly smile at his mother who returns his massacred dinner and promptly hurl the rest of it at her with the other hand! Gradually he will begin to show a preference for using one hand and this in turn will help establish his laterality so that he becomes right- or left-handed.

By the time he is eighteen months old, he lifts the cup to his mouth and drinks well but is still rather messy with the spoon. He is continuing to learn to do more for himself. He takes off his gloves and socks and undoes any zips on his clothes and tries to put on his shoes. He has a vocabulary of ten words and asks for a drink or something to eat by name, 'mih' (milk), 'bikky' (biscuit).

The toddler is concerned with himself and the here and now of his existence. He is learning to be a person in his own right and he wanders off from his mother to explore and test his environment. At the same time he needs to be reassured that his mother is within reach so he pops back every so often just to make sure. He is a passionate explorer at this age, poking his fingers into all sorts of nooks and crannies, taking out the pots and pans and putting them into each other or filling them with spoons, bricks, potatoes or whatever objects happen to be within reach. During his first twelve months of life, he has been learning by looking and listening and later by touching and holding things and getting the taste and feel of them by putting them in his mouth.

Now his newly acquired skill to walk and the strength of his urge to explore help him to find out more about his world. He tries out new ways of doing things. He may try walking down the stairs, holding on to the bannister rail and half way down, turn round and crawl down backwards the rest of the way. He is an eager beaver, discovering what size and shape objects are, whether they move or not. He is awake for more of the day and busy, busy, busy. The strength of this urge to explore and the fact that he becomes fully mobile and is insatiably curious, are mainly the reasons for the trouble in which he finds himself. He has got an idea of his own desires and individuality and when he's thwarted he knows it and feels angry. When his mother refuses to let him touch the electric fire or pull the television flex he may react by yelling in anger and kicking the floor in rage.

During the second year of life, he is changing as he is maturing and one of these changes is the way in which he expresses his feelings. A little baby who is hungry feels furious with the whole world. A one-year-old may slap his mother's face (if she lets him) when he's very cross. The eighteen-month-old is quite likely to lie on the floor, kicking and screaming with rage when he feels thwarted.

The psychiatrist Erik Erikson[2] notes a crisis of development during fifteen months to four years when the child is fully mobile, wants to do many things which he is physically incapable of doing or which may be harmful to him. The crux for parents is letting him explore but ensuring that he doesn't do himself damage or wreck the house in the process. The child doesn't realise what can happen as a result of his actions since he is too young to link cause and effect. But he must learn that there are some things he cannot do. He doesn't realise that throwing books into the fire or banging the T.V. with a hammer are dangerous pastimes. Luckily during the second year of life he is extremely distractible and can be lured away from some dangerous situation to an equally interesting safe one without the wear and tear for mother and child of a confrontation. It's worth remembering that he's learning by exploring and that he has to test his own skills before he can advance to the next stage.

This exploratory process extends to speech as well. He is reaching a peak in the stage of jargon, which is probably more important for his speech and language development than people realise.

JARGON

At about eighteen months of age, the toddler's speech activity consists of a few meaningful words, some vocal play usually when he is alone, some repetition of adult words if they are introduced naturally into the child's vocal play, and a great deal of what can be called jargon. This sounds like paragraphs of gibberish which occur as a running commentary during the toddler's exploratory activities. He may commence a flow of jargon as he opens a cupboard, pause while he takes out and examines a brick, resume his jabbering while he toddles off to the laundry basket into which he drops the brick, hopefully retrievable before it banjaxes the washing machine.

The gap between the child's attempts to say his first words and the flow of adult speech is bridged by the use of jargon. He usually passes through the jargon stage by the age of two years. The eighteen-month-old may repeat parrot-wise words or phrases he hears. This probably occurs occasionally with all toddlers but is more marked in some cases. An adult could say, 'There's Mrs. O'Reilly', and the child may repeat, 'O'Reilly'; or again a mother searching frantically for the car keys could say, 'I'll kill your father for taking the keys!', and get quite a start to hear her toddler repeat, 'Kill father taking keys'! This echo-like speech is a normal stage in a young child's language development. He passes through it quite rapidly and it is seldom heard after two-and-a-half years. By the time he is twenty-one months, the child has a twenty word vocabulary, and he may begin to use two-word phrases. When a part of a doll or teddy is named, he can point to that part. If his mother says, 'eyes' he can point to his own or teddy's eyes. He can hold his cup well, lifting it to his lips, drinking from it and replacing it on the table without spilling.

FIRST PHRASES

The next milestone in the young child's speech and language development is when he starts putting words together to form his first phrases. At about twenty-four months jargon is fading and being gradually replaced by the child's first sentences which can be simple such as 'All gone' or 'Dada bye bye' or more sophisticated such as 'me show book'. He is starting to string words together meaningfully.

Much of what he says will not at this stage be pronounced clearly of course. The play materials and activities which capture his interest around this time can be used to stimulate his vocabulary. During his second year of life he likes games in which one object is placed inside another, where heaps of bricks are built up and then knocked over, emptying and filling games. He likes games in which objects are pushed and pulled, lids or doors opened and shut. In fact he likes any activity that stimulates his curiosity. Talking to him about what he is doing can help him to learn new words. As he knocks over his pile of bricks with a gleeful shout, say 'All fall down' for example or 'Bricks fall down' or 'Down'. One of his favourite toys at this stage is likely to be a cart or truck which he can load and unload, push and pull. As he is pushing it say 'push your cart'.

At twenty-four months he will probably enjoy playing alone but near adults. He is increasingly interested in copying what adults do and will use a toy telephone, sweep the floor and perform other activities in imitation of his parents. He is trying to do more for himself and helps to pull up and down his pants while being dressed and thrusts his arms into the armholes of his clothes. He washes and dries his hands and body (after a fashion) and holds his mug in one hand as he drinks. He is well able to feed himself with only moderate spilling. About this time he will probably be gaining more control and making strides in the area of toilet training.

His store of words is growing and he may well be using two hundred recognisable words. He joins in nursery rhymes and songs, often supplying the missing word. His mother can say 'Humpty Dumpty sat on a ————' and the child may supply the missing word 'wall'. He can recognise people and familiar activities when he sees them pictured in books. He becomes more aware of a sense of personal possession and can become passionately attached to a favourite toy or blanket, which becomes his constant companion. Woe betide the offender who tries to grab a possession from a two-year-old. He is liable to get a bang on the head for his sins! The child's present store of words must increase to keep pace with his growing needs. He already names something that interests him and adds a word to it by way of comment. 'Mama up' he may say when he wants to be lifted up or 'milk gone' when he has finished drinking his milk. He will next learn to speak of the way in which two things relate to each other and use a verb or a word used as a verb — 'Pussy hurt Baby' or again 'Mama go bye bye'. He needs to qualify what he says so that his exact meaning can be understood. He will need to learn to add prepositions and to formulate his curiosity by asking questions. He will need to learn how to express plurals and gender and past and future tenses.

The following examples of phrases used between twenty-four and thirty-six months will give an idea of how a child's language grows during this time.

Twenty-five-and-a-half months:
'Where go?'; 'Do again'; 'Big Box'.

Twenty-eight-and-a-half months:
'Is it car?'; 'I want see car'; 'I will read book'.

Thirty months:
'I very tall'; 'I drawing dog'; 'In big box'.

Thirty and-a-half months:
'I show you the book'; 'It goes in the box'; 'I do not want apple'.

Thirty-two months:
'I will not do that again'; 'Where shall I go?'; 'I don't want an apple'.

Thirty-five and-a-half months:
'I will read a book'; 'I will show you the book'.

In the period between twenty-four and thirty-six months, the child is working hard to decide things for himself and to resist pressures from other people. The balkiness of the one-year-old takes on a new form. Where the one-year-old contradicted his mother, the two-and-a-half year-old even contradicts himself! He may decide he wants to go into the garden with his coat, wellingtons and gloves on, only to be very determined after three minutes in the garden about coming inside again, which involves a full undress rehearsal.

As one mother put it, 'His first word was no', and the phrase most often heard when he was two-and-a-half years was, 'No, No, No!' The two-and-a-half year-old gets furious if someone interferes in a job he is doing or rearranges his belongings. It can take a lot of patience on the part of parents to accept this negative phase. It's worth remembering that the child is trying to tie up his experiences and make sense of them in terms of his present skills.

The whole problem of grammar is a challenge to the child. At the same time he has an increasing need to enlarge his vocabulary. It is scarcely a cause of wonder if he stumbles over his words at this stage.

As the child nears his third birthday he has much to learn. He is full of energy and meets taboos and frustrations at every turn. He must learn to be a social being whether he wants to or not. He has a tremendous need to express himself so that he can be understood, have answers to his questions, and express his emotions. Increasing his vocabulary and using his newly learnt words are of paramount importance. Not only does he learn new words but he needs to use them in a grammatical form which can carry his exact meaning. Added to this he is trying to copy the pattern of speech fluency he hears in his environment.

Between twelve and thirty-six months the child has a lot of learning to do and he can be helped with his language progress. Some parents are instinctive in this regard. However, many of us may need to learn a bit ourselves in order to help effectively.

ESSENTIAL FACTORS

In order that a child learns to talk, some basic factors are necessary. It is helpful to know what these factors are and to make sure they are present before expecting a child's speech and language to develop and progress.

To be able to talk in phrases at about twenty-four months a child needs to be of average intelligence. A child with lower than average intelligence will probably require special help to promote his speech development. The child needs to be able to hear the sounds of speech before we can expect him to reproduce the words and phrases spoken in his home. He must hear these sounds loudly enough and often enough. He also needs to be equipped with a speech apparatus that works adequately.

If a child had a cleft palate, this would have to be considered when looking at his speech progress. He needs to be able to move correctly the muscles used for speech. The child also needs to have a balanced emotional and environmental development. He must *want* to talk and this factor can be affected by the type of speech environment in which he finds himself.

The helpful speech environment is one in which the child realises that speech is meaningful. He needs to discover that the noises spoken by other people have a meaning and that he can influence others by making these useful noises. He won't be able to do this if he doesn't frequently hear people talking to each other and to him. The mother who talks to her baby is helping him to acquire language. As well as listening to and understanding speech used meaningfully, the child needs plenty of opportunity to *practice* the sounds, syllables, words and phrases of speech. He needs to listen to his own attempts at speech. If he is constantly bombarded by stimuli, he may not be able to do this effectively.

He also needs to be able to *use* his speech. In the helpful speech environment, his parents can make sure this occurs by expecting a speech response from the child at the level of his speech development. The 'helpful' elder sister who speaks for her two-year-old brother is not only depriving him of opportunities to use speech but may also give him the impression that he needn't bother to talk as she'll do it for him! He needs to be encouraged to talk without being pushed and with no anxiety on the part of his parents. An anxious attitude towards the child's speech may in fact have the undesired effect of hindering his speech progress.

The child needs to reproduce sounds and with encouragement will progress to say words, and by the time he is two years has the idea that everything has a name. He will be encouraged to use speech if he is able to do so, and if he realises how useful and what fun talking is. Speech development can become unsettled or perhaps interrupted by illness, emotional disturbance and even the birth of a new baby.

Any child with a special problem such as mental handicap, cerebral palsy, deafness, will of course need special help. Professional advice can be given while the child is very young. A baby with a hearing loss can be helped significantly even during the early months of life. The child with special problems also needs to be helped in a specific way at home and parents can make sure he gets this particular help by seeking expert advice as soon as possible.

The phrase most often heard at
two-and-a-half years is, 'No! No! No!'

Guidelines

Make sure your child is motivated so that he will *want* to talk.

Encourage him to enjoy sounds, words and phrases in pleasurable situations, e.g. bath time.

Help him to build his vocabulary by naming objects as he plays with and touches them.

Talk to him clearly and simply about simple pictures of familiar objects.

Use walks to the shops and visits to friends as opportunities to help his language growth.

Expect a language response from your child in keeping with his level of speech development.

Is he right- or left-handed? Give him the chance to find out.

Do not demand too high a standard of speech from your child.

Do not ask your toddler to show off his speech or force him to talk to strangers.

Do not correct your child's speech.

Do not expect words to be correctly pronounced at this stage.

Use toys and books suitable for his age to stimulate the growth of language such as hammer and pegs set, posting box, toy telephone etc.

Bear in mind that speech and language development are individual.

Seek professional advice if your child is not talking *at all* or if you are concerned about his speech progress.

Consult your family doctor or local health clinic if you suspect special problems such as hearing loss, backwardness in your child.

3
The Pre-School Child

3

The Pre-School Child

THE PRE-SCHOOL CHILD, unless he is handicapped has learned to sit, stand, walk, and feed himself after a fashion. He has been forming a relationship with his family. During the pre-school years (from the time he is two-and-a-half 'till he starts school), he will be consolidating what he has been learning earlier and he will be constantly adding to that experience as he continues to develop physically, emotionally, mentally and socially. He is beginning to mix with children of his own age group and starting to strike out on his own. Life is full of exploration and not a few pitfalls. On one side he is ready and eager for life and what it offers, and on the other, the effort involved in seeking independence outside the home often results in negative and frustrated behaviour. Play can afford him the opportunity to express his emotions and is a valuable learning experience.

The pre-school child is starting to become a person in his own right and is learning to get on with other people. He is developing his imagination, powers of reasoning and he needs outlets to express his emotions. He is also getting a sense of enjoyment and achievement from learning to mix and share with his age group in play situations.

PERIOD OF NON FLUENCY

The pre-school child who is becoming involved in stringing his new words into sentences can usually be expected to hesitate a lot in the process. Many children experience a period of non-fluency which is quite *normal* at this stage and should be accepted as such. A child will stumble while learning to walk, so we can expect the child to stumble over his speech while he is learning to talk. Little children cannot be expected to achieve the fluency of adult speech before they are able. While the child is trying to master fluent speech, he is also making definite efforts to be independent of his mother outside the home and is starting to mix with his own age group. He is becoming more aware of what he wants to say and do and at the same time his social survival depends, among other things, on how he learns to control and modify his behaviour. He is thinking, doing and learning through play.

This is a very busy time for the child's speech and language development. He needs time to think of what he wants to say and time to say it. There is a difference between non-fluency and actual stammering. The child passing through a period of non-fluency will say:

'Can I can - can - can - can - can I go with you?' while the child who is stammering will say:

'C-c-c-c-c-can I guh-guh-guh- go w-with yy-y-y-you?'

The child who is non-fluent shows most of his hesitancy in *organising* what he wants to say,

38

whereas the child who is stammering has difficulty in *speaking* his thoughts to people.

The child in a period of non-fluency needs a speech environment where his hesitations — 'Can I, can-can-can-can-can I go-go-go with you Mama?' — are accepted as signs of a normal period of non-fluency, which they are. It is important for the child that parents do not become anxious about his speech or focus on it. The child needs a standard of fluency to follow which is within his reach so that he won't feel frustrated by trying to achieve a degree of fluency beyond his present capacity. He needs to hear short simple phrases and words, the meanings of which he understands, used simply and often. If in doubt about your child's speech fluency (the rhythmic flow of speech) it is well to consult a speech therapist for advice.

LANGUAGE GROWTH

The child's language has developed from his first attempts to say a meaningful word to quite a sophisticated level. He is still developing language and will continue to do so for quite a time yet. The few words he has learnt as an infant no longer serve him so the pre-school child starts gathering a vocabulary to suit his present needs.

By the time he is three, his large vocabulary includes plurals and pronouns. He is able to discriminate between things of different sizes and he can understand taking turns. He can name drawings and can repeat a sentence of seven syllables. About this time he starts to acquire a sense of sex identity and can tell male from female. He eats and drinks with minimal mess and rarely needs help. He is more or less toilet trained. By this time he will usually have established a preference for which hand he is going to use.

He is busy learning new words and loses no chance of finding out: 'who that?', 'what's that called?' etc. He chats in a monologue mainly about present happenings but also about the past and make-believe situations. He is getting a grasp of how sentences are put together. This know-how helps him to convey the exact meaning of what he wants to say. He is working hard at using prepositions correctly as we can see from these comments made by a girl of three years and three months.

'She was very good of making pictures'.

'I couldn't go out, I have only on my socks'.

It is commonly accepted that girls talk earlier than boys. It is also an interesting fact that speech defects are more common in boys than in girls. The incidence of stammering has been given as 3 to 1, boy versus girls, and as high as 8 to 1 has been quoted[3].

The early pre-school age is the age of rhythm. As a baby he will have clapped his hands, as much a social gesture as an experiment in co-ordination. Gradually he has been gaining more control until he reaches the stage where he claps or moves in rhythm to a song or nursery rhyme. Now he listens eagerly to stories, songs and rhymes and demands his favourites over and over again. He knows several nursery rhymes and he will make up his own nonsense rhymes. Songs with actions are loved by the child at this age. They can also help his language growth and natural sense of rhythm.

'I'm a little teapot, short and stout,

Here's my handle, here's my spout.

When I am ready, I will shout

'Tip me up and pour me out'.

This example from the Ladybird series is accompanied by a picture of a teapot and a picture of the child acting the rhyme.

Singing or saying these rhymes for the child, and later with him, is something both parents and child can enjoy. By the time the child is four years old, he has a grasp of the grammatical rules used in his environment. He uses past tenses and conjunctions: because, although. He can tell opposites and can define words. He can discriminate more and grasp similarities and differences. He can understand prepositions and such concepts as sleepy and cold. Of course he doesn't always use every preposition correctly and his words will sometimes sound confused as he can mix up syllables, so that we may hear 'chingel' for 'children' or 'demember' for 'remember'.

At four he is able to dress and undress with little help and can wash and dry his face and hands and wash his teeth. By the time he is five, he can be expected to use descriptive words spontaneously, know colours and the chief parts of the body by name. He can count to ten and repeat three digits after hearing them spoken. He can also be expected to know comparatives and common opposites — big, small, hard, soft. His vocabulary can consist of two thousand words which can be doubled by the time he is seven.

Each child has his own age of speech readiness which varies enormously from child to child. Therefore it is futile for parents to compare the speech progress of one child with that of another. Nonsense rhymes and monologues give the pre-school child opportunity to explore and experiment with the new parts of grammar he is learning. He likes making up his own nonsense rhymes like this one made up by a three-and-a-half-year-old:

Saucey jam jam

Saucey jam jam

Will you go in your boat?

Saucey jam jam

Will you eat your eggs in your boat?

Saucey eats his egg in the boat

Saucey jam jam.

Here is a monologue which involves the repeated use of past tenses:

Skoppi hop once went for a walk, and he stealed some lollipops and he stealed some people and he stealed the shopkeeper's things and then he went home. He just give the money to the lady. He singed a song 'pflo, pflo mishen!' He was rolled over and he runned in the middle of the road.

The pre-school child experiments not only with the way sentences are put together but also with the way the words in his new vocabulary are pronounced. We don't expect him to pronounce every word clearly at this stage. There are some children speaking perfectly clearly at four-and-a-half-years-old while other may not master S and SH sounds till the sixth year and R sound till the seventh year[4].

It's helpful to remember that the child who is

learning to talk is not engaged in frivolity. He is in fact working and working hard. He can get great fun from the effort. Just as a baby crows with delight at the long streams of sound he is babbling, so the pre-school child enjoys getting the feel and listening to the sound and rhythm of words and phrases. He weaves groups of like-sounding words through his rhymes, monologues and stories.

Skoppy hoop came along. Plinky is his marry, tally, tacky. Scooby Doo was tired and then he went to bed. (Three years)

Saying and listening to words which sound alike but are not identical helps the child to pick out the similarities and differences between the words.

Hoppity Hop, Hoppity Hop

Hoppity Hop, Hoppity Hop

Poppity Pop

In the snow the snowmans go

I like laughing laughing,

lappy, snappy, and happy appy jakky.

(Four years)

He is learning to discriminate between like-sounding words and experimenting with new ways of pronouncing these words. The following is a typical example and was said with pronounced rhythm:

Don't bounce en ever be there again

Ever, never, under, tell, under yell

Shell, tell. Dogs in the richard

Over the ballet

The pre-school child likes to 'read' books, like this four-year-old who 'read':

They were liffing, laughing and they were spitting, hissing and kissing.

This child of three years and ten months 'read' the picture book story 'Goldilocks and The Three Bears' as follows:

Why is her mother brushing her hair?

Oh yes! — to get out the tangles.

Was she late to have her breakfast?

Oh yes! — we're like three bears

We had porridge for our breakfast

Oh *yes*!! We *are* the three bears!!

He looked his bowl and he had none porridge left.

Poor, poor baby bear! Did his only porridge cool quickly?

Here they are in the woods. Is that baby bear? — that's mother bear, is that mother bear?

Father bear has the most sticks. Why do they have to catch sticks? Cos they need the porridge cooked.

Oh yes — mother needs her carrying her sticks and her porridge warm. Then the three bears saw Goldilocks in the bed. Then mother said 'Don't go to the forest any more'.

The above was related with animated expression. We can see from the number of questions asked that it is no wonder this is the age of...

44

QUESTIONS, QUESTIONS, QUESTIONS

During the pre-school years, the child is exploring and discovering the world about him. Asking questions is one interesting way in which he finds out the how, where, when and why of life. The questions can be simple: 'What's that?' or profound –

Why do cats kill mouses?

Little mouses small and friendly

They no hurt cats

(Three-and-a-half years)

The questioning reaches a peak at the four-year-old level when almost every utterance the child makes is a question.

Why is Daddy going to the shops?

Why is he getting the paper?

Is he going at Friday on football?

Why does God turn on the taps all the time?

These questions are asked and then often answered by the child himself (as in the story of Goldilocks and The Three Bears). He keeps up a running commentary on the subject and while his busy mother breaks off from her activities to answer one of his questions, he has run on to the next item of interest.

Sure you don't wash shoes? I never wash shoes, only tending (pretending) ones made of plastic – sure plastic doesn't break?

The pre-school child talks about anything and everything. The subjects of birth, sex, dreams, fears and fantasies often come in for discussion or comment.

In my dream I growed bigly up to thirteen, one three-year and ten-month-old told her mother, and then I grow fallee little, little, little — I didn't know who was dehind me.

About the same time, that child also commented,

The mummies and daddies get the babies in the mummies' tummies but God is in real charge.

On hearing of the death of a relative, a four-year-old remarked,
Oh yes — she's gone to a new world
Oh yes — a blue and white world.

The range of topics discussed is infinite. Language is used by the child as a useful and enriching means of expression. For instance, everyday details:
I'm the great eater of swisseroll, you know, I'm even a great eater of chocolate swisseroll.
(four years)

Comments can be totally unexpected as this one from a four-year-old, sick in bed, who told her mother:
Chingel (children) don't pinch mothers when they're sick!

The child uses language to express emotion.

When I smile at you, when you smile at me, I just kiss you.
(Four years)

Often the child's sense of humour weaves in and out of his phrases:

I just can't sleep with meself laughing in bed!
(Four years)

The pre-school child is starting to separate fact

from fantasy. He tells long stories sometimes confusing the two. He chats about and acts out make-believe situations. Here are some comments by a four-year-old on the subject —

1. Pleests (a word for priests and police) are a people. Fairies be in fairyland.

2. Witches can't go in shops cos the people will be scared. Witches be in witches land. This is peoples land.

3. I flushed the witches down the toilet. No, they won't come back cos they love being lonely in the toilets!

4. Bad witches could climb up mountains and friken (frighten) God — if they brang their broons (broomsticks).

The child's spontaneous and imaginative use of language is an enriching experience for himself and for those in his surroundings. He needs to talk as much as he needs to breathe. He needs to express what has happened, what he wishes to and fears may happen. The child is dependent on the people about him, his family and other children and later, on teachers and neighbours. The child also depends on his fantasy equivalents of these people in his inner world. It is not only what 'they' do to him in reality but the role in which he casts them which determines how they affect him. He can use play to act out real and imaginary situations including his fears and fantasies. Let's take a look at the importance of play in the life of the pre-school child.

PLAY

Play is a vital part of the learning process for young children. When the child is playing he is in fact learning to grow and develop. Play is coming to terms with life on a physical, intellectual and social level.

To start with, the pre-school child will prefer to play by himself even if other people are present. It will take time and some maturity before he is able to play *with* his own age group for any length of time. This situation can be encouraged by having a small group of children meeting regularly under the care of one or two adults, or alternatively the child could attend a playgroup.

Play is not only a valuable learning experience but can also provide a situation in which the child will *want* to talk. Let's look at some of the aspects of play which will be most helpful in promoting speech and language growth. It is beyond the scope of this book to go into detail about all the fascinating aspects of play and the pre-school child. **Clear, Colourful Pictures** to be looked at and talked about are one way of encouraging language. The pictures should be large and vivid and, to start with, familiar to the child. Describing the picture simply will give the child a pattern of fluency to follow which is within his capacity. 'This is a picture of the sea-side. Here's a girl swimming in the sea. The boy is playing in the sand. A man is digging in the sand with a spade.' Soon the child will want to talk about the picture himself. **Rhymes, Jingles and Finger Play** are another aspect of play which encourage language along with a sense of rhythm and enjoyment. The child will enjoy the repetition of sounds and words which, as shown earlier, is an important part of his speech development. **Make Believe Play** is another aspect of play which can be used to help the pre-school child's language. The child needs to talk not only about the here and now but also the past, what might happen and what he wishes or fears may happen. By dressing up as well as acting out real life characters and situations in play e.g. shopping, mummies and daddies, doctor and hospital and school, the child can express his ideas of what these situations mean to him. Quite often a shy child will join in games with one or two others if the element of dressing up or talking on the telephone is introduced.

Visits to the zoo and the seaside can be re-enacted. Make believe play gives scope to the child to *talk* about all sorts of facts and fantasies of his everyday life. He can pretend to be a father, a mother, a policeman, a fireman, a baby, a doctor, a nurse, a bus driver, a teacher, in the free atmosphere of a play situation. He will want to talk about his roles and because of this will feel the need to learn relevant words and sentences so that he can communicate his ideas and feelings to others. A 'home corner' in the playroom or kitchen could be the stimulus a child needs for make believe play. The home corner could have a box with clothes for dressing up, some household equipment e.g. brush and dustpan, cups and saucers and tray, telephone (two intercom telephones are useful), doll's pram and cot. A card table with a blanket over the top and sides gives a sense of privacy to the home for two or three children who can have tea parties 'inside' away from adults. The larger the home corner the better but for most households space is at a premium so an easily erected and collapsible 'House' is probably the answer.

MUSIC AND DRAMA

Through music, musical movement and drama, the pre-school child can gain valuable experience in expressing his ideas and emotions in terms of movement, mime, language and movement. A good sense of rhythm can be developed along with his natural sense of enjoyment associated with sounds, melodies, movement and words.

BOOKS

The large range of colourful books available now which can help the pre-school child's language development is exciting and encouraging. By listening to stories read aloud, the child can be helped to increase his vocabulary in a relaxed atmosphere. By helping to make up stories about fact and fiction, he can develop his imagination.

By hearing a story read over and over again, he can become familiar with words and grammar and at the same time get a pattern of fluency to follow. The pre-school child enjoys funny stories, repetitive stories and stories with a chorus like 'The Gingerbread Man' and 'The Three Bears'. Stories with pictures appeal to the child as do stories which widen the child's knowledge and experience of life. Many situations, going to hospital, going to school, the birth of a new baby, travel, the zoo, the circus, can be introduced to the child in story form, and at the same time provide opportunity for discussion. A story about going to hospital can enable the child to ask questions:

'Are there other children in hospital?' and to express his fears, 'Is it dark at night in hospital?'

A suggested list of books that stretch the child's ability, and stimulate his interest in broader fields, as well as books giving factual information can be found in the appendix at the end of this book.

Many of these books can be borrowed from the Library. Apart from books which tell stories and stimulate the child and widen his experience of the world about him, there are specific play and learn Activity Books specially geared to help the pre-school child make his own discoveries and to form concepts. Activity books are specially designed for the under-fives and are packed with activities such as cutting out, matching shapes, stitching, colouring etc. These books can be regarded as a worthwhile extra to the usual toys, and everyday objects surrounding the child. The activities are a lively topic for conversation between adult and child. By taking about what he is doing and receiving comments and answers, the child can formulate his ideas, clarify his thoughts and extend his vocabulary.

PLAYGROUPS

A good playgroup provides an outlet for creativity, promotes social intercourse, encourages the development of speech and language and meets needs in the young child which might not otherwise be satisfied. Many parents have started their own small playgroups. So, if you feel that way inclined, do forge ahead and explore the possibilities. To start your own playgroup or for information about playgroups, you should contact your nearest pre-school playgroup association.

One of the helpful leaflets from the Irish Pre-School Playgroup Association states: 'Playgroups create an environment where learning can take place. The emphasis is on the total development of the child and the old idea of teaching children by instruction, repetition and memory is replaced by providing a good atmosphere, good materials and the freedom to investigate and explore. There is therefore no formal teaching, no reading, writing or arithmetic; these three Rs are replaced by the three Ps: play, paint, playdough. A varied range of equipment is provided for all kinds of play, creative/imaginative, social, adventure, constructive and even destructive. The basic essentials are sand, water, paint, modelling material, building material — good story and picture books, material for active adventure play, opportunity for family play, provision for musical activities, manipulative play materials'.

The learning of the pre-school child comes largely from being involved in ordinary everyday affairs. Most of his time is spent playing. At this stage play is learning and learning is play. For example the child who is messily playing soothing games with water and sand can also learn something of how water obeys its own laws and about the effect of water on sand. The child can get an idea of number in the broad sense by putting as many acorns as there are saucers and spoons on a table. By placing for instance five of these objects side by side he can learn that five is a definite number and what it means.

The pre-school child who is talking very little or the child whose speech isn't readily understood can be helped by attending a small playgroup. It is a mistake to keep a child from a playgroup because he doesn't seem to be speaking as well or as much as others of his age.

Mixing with other pre-school children in the stimulating atmosphere of a playgroup can often be just what the child needs.

Make-believe play helps speech and language development.

Guidelines

THE PRE-SCHOOL CHILD

Talk to your pre-school child in simple sentences.

Make time to listen to what he has to say.

Use real life situations to help his speech progress, talking to him about daily home activities, shopping, etc.

Visits and outings, the Park, Zoo, etc. can all be useful situations *provided* you use speech in connection with them.

Make sure he is able to mix with his own age group in play situations.

Consider the possibility of a playgroup for him.

Read him familiar stories to help build his vocabulary.

Show him objects as you name them.

Do not correct his speech at this stage even if you are itching to do so!

Use some of the books available as an extra to the child's everyday toys and activities.

Use rhymes, jingles and finger play to encourage his speech development.

Make opportunity at home for the child to engage in make-believe play.

Make sure he gets opportunities to express his emotions and to 'let off steam'.

Remember that the child can gain valuable experience in expression through listening to and playing music, singing, musical movement and drama.

Listen to *what* your child says not how he says it.

Do not press the child to recite or sing in company. Expression should *never* be forced.

Do not set too high a speech standard for him to follow.

Do not rush or interrupt the child while he is talking.

Remember that anxiety does not help and can in fact hinder his speech fluency.

Make sure the child is not teased or mocked because of the way he talks.

Do not allow brothers or sisters to speak for the child or interrupt or correct his speech.

Remember that a stage of non-fluency is not a stammer — seek advice if in doubt about this.

Do not focus on a child's speech during a period of non-fluency — instead, talk simply to the child giving him a speech standard to follow that is within his capacity.

Consult a speech therapist if your pre-school child is not talking *at all*, if he is not putting words together by thirty-six months or if you are concerned about his speech progress.

Try not to be influenced by remarks made about

your child's speech.

Seek help if your child seems to have a special problem like hearing loss, physical or mental handicap, etc.

Have recurring ear, nose and throat problems such as 'runny ears' medically checked.

4
What Influences A Child's Speech?

Environment
School
Hospitalisation
Stress

4
What Influences A Child's Speech?

WE HAVE SEEN earlier the basic factors which are essential for the development of speech and language. There are many factors which influence a child's speech while he is learning to talk. Let's look briefly at some of them.

ENVIRONMENT

The effects of environment on a young child's developing speech and language are significant. The child who hasn't any special problems (such as backwardness, hearing loss) will usually develop his linguistic skills with a sense of fun and achievement if he hears spoken speech, and is encouraged to make efforts at communicating verbally. The child who is not talked to, who spends the day alone in his bedroom, alone in his pram at the end of the garden, who is not stimulated so that he will *want* to talk, can find difficulty in developing speech and language.

A good speech environment is one in which the parents *play* with the child *using speech*. The baby and young child must learn that talking has a meaning and that by talking he can express his wants and have his needs satisfied. The child needs to realise how valuable and enriching language can be. The young baby who yells loudly for attention, ceasing his heart-rending roars the instant he is picked up and hugged by his mother, only to start an agonising wail the moment he is put back in his cot, is a good example of someone using his voice to express what he wants!

Hearing people using speech conversationally in the home helps the young child realise how important and pleasurable talking can be. While emphasising the importance of stimulating the child to develop speech and language, over-concern or anxiety will not help and can indeed hinder the child's speech progress. Pressing the child to 'show off' his speech to visitors, correcting and interrupting his speech may in fact make the child self-conscious about the way he talks and give him the impression that talking is something to be anxious about.

As a young child will react to his parents' efforts to encourage him to talk, so also will he react to feelings of anxiety on their part. He may feel a sense of urgency to speak more quickly and more clearly and may try to achieve a greater mastery of fluency and articulation than he is ready for. More than anything, he needs to be allowed to develop at his own rate, to speak at his own pace and in his own way. As mentioned earlier, if there is doubt about his speech progress, professional advice can be sought.

Correcting the child's speech may seem to many parents a sensible thing to do. A conscientious mother may for example say, 'Don't say chain, say train dear', feeling that she is helping the child. In fact quite often the opposite is the case. The young child has to listen to and sort out the different sounds in a word and the sequence of the syllables *before* he can be expected to pronounce it clearly. Correcting him can in fact confuse him. If he mispronounces a word, you could show him the object, while you name it clearly and without fuss.

Much discussion has taken place regarding the advisability of using 'baby talk' to children. Sometimes the use of 'doggy' for dog or 'horsey' for horse can help the child to hear the G sound at the end of dog and the S sound at the end of horse. The child, as he matures, will drop the Y sound from 'doggy' and 'horsey' and be aware that the sounds G and S are an essential part of 'dog' and 'horse'. Personally, I don't feel it matters whether baby talk is used or not, *provided* it is in keeping with the child's level of speech development. The child himself will usually discard earlier forms of expression as he outgrows them.

A good speech environment encourages but doesn't urge the child to talk. The child needs a standard of speech to follow which is neither too high nor too low for his ability. He needs to hear speech spoken reasonably clearly and reasonably slowly. Speaking in clear simple sentences gives the child a pattern of speech to follow which is within his capacity. He needs to be encouraged, not forced to talk, to be praised naturally, not excessively, for his efforts. Above all he needs to enjoy learning to talk in a stimulating and unhurried atmosphere.

SCHOOL

After parents, teachers are perhaps the people most closely connected with the child's speech and language, and the influence of teachers and school on a child's speech is very considerable indeed. School is a social situation where the child can be encouraged to develop and grow socially, intellectually and emotionally. Meeting children of his own age group will give him the opportunity to share and communicate with them on a grander scale than he did at home in his pre-school years.

His teacher is of vital importance to him and among her myriad tasks is the significant one of stimulating him to increase his vocabulary and powers of expression. By the time the child is five years-old, he can be expected to use descriptive words spontaneously, know colours and the chief parts of the body by name. He can be expected to know comparatives and common opposites: big-small, hard-soft.

His first teacher is a big influence in the young child's life and can do much to help his speech by providing situations where free expression is encouraged in an unhurried atmosphere. For instance, the teacher who listens to the child's news is giving the child the essential experience of being able to talk at his own pace and in his own way without fear of correction or interruption. Drama, music, musical movement, can all be used successfully in the school situation to help develop rhythm and language and to promote expression and self-confidence.

If a child needs help with his speech it is a good idea to contact the teacher to explain exactly what the situation is. In my experience, teachers are only too willing to help a particular child once they are aware of how best to help. Teachers cannot possibly be expected to assess and treat speech problems. They can and do help children with these problems. To help, they must first know that the problem exists, the extent of it and the type of specific help needed at each stage. For instance, the young child with temporary hearing loss associated with recurring ear, nose, throat infections can be helped at school *if* the teacher is aware of the problem. The child can be placed at the front of the class so that he doesn't have to strain to hear. One of the most important things a teacher can do is to show by her *attitude* that she understands and accepts the way a child talks. This means allowing the child time to talk without correction or interruption.

Teachers can also help by discussing any apparent speech problem with a child's parents, perhaps suggesting that professional advice can be sought if there is a doubt about a particular child's speech progress. In the case of a child who is attending a speech therapist, contact is essential between the speech therapist and the teacher so that both are working along the same lines to help the child. Some children with speech problems have difficulty in learning to read. Some of these children may be Dyslexic, which means that there is a problem in interpreting the visual symbols, the actual letters and words.

Mirror writing, that is writing which makes sense if reflected in a mirror, can occur. Others may be able to interpret the words and letters but for one of many reasons, may not be making reading progress. The remedial reading teacher and the speech therapist work in close co-operation where a child has speech and reading difficulties. It is important that reading difficulties be recognised as such and professionally assessed. In the case of a child requiring special help from a speech therapist or remedial teacher, the interest and help of the child's school teacher is not only appreciated, but essential if the child is to maintain progress.

HOSPITAL

Hospitals can mean different things to young children. The child can associate it with his mother's absence and the birth of a new baby, or perhaps with his own experience of being in hospital. Hospitalisation can be an experience from which he can benefit or it may have a traumatic effect. It is significant that some children with speech disturbance have a history of hospitalisation which occurred around the same time as the onset of the speech disturbance. Hospitalisation, while not experienced by all children, can affect the speech of some children and for this reason I have included it here.

There are hospitals which encourage the mother to sleep in the hospital beside her sick child. I have had two children hospitalised for surgery and have availed of this service. Both children left the hospital with reluctance! The nursing staff were aware of a mother's feelings, and welcomed the help parents could give looking after the needs of the children. We had on both occasions a small cheerful 'room' which gave us privacy and at the same time was part of the ward. When the time came for surgery, all the children walked with their teddys and dolls to the operating theatre (no trolleys). Parents who wished could accompany children as far as the waiting room.

I give this personal experience as I feel it shows that (a) hospitalisation for the young child does *not* have to be associated with trauma and that

(b) there are some enlightened hospitals where mothers or fathers can stay with a sick child. Of course it isn't always possible or necessary for a child to have his mother there all the time.

As soon as it is known that a child is to be hospitalised, talking to him about the hospital *in general* can be a help. There is a useful Ladybird book with pictures of hospital activities, ambulances, nurses and new babies, and children reading in bed. It is a good idea to consider the possibility of staying with the child if he is under seven. If this can be arranged, the whole procedure will be less strange to the child. However in every case it is not feasible or advisable perhaps for a parent to stay with a child in hospital. Obviously it would be impossible to stay with a long-stay patient. It can be distressing to come round after an operation in a strange bed wearing someone else's clothes — so, packing the child's familiar toys and his own pyjamas will help bring something of home into the hospital. The child needs to have the situation explained shortly before he goes into hospital so that he knows what to expect. For example, 'We'll be sleeping in a bedroom together (if this is so) and the other children will be sleeping near us". He needs to know that the doctor with whom he should have a friendly relationship, will take out the tonsils or adenoids when the child is asleep. He needs to know that when he wakes up, his throat or nose will be sore for a while but that the soreness will go away. It is important that the child should realise why he will be feeling sick, groggy or sore, and that this condition will be temporary. If your child has to be hospitalised bring him to the hospital yourself. Have a chat with the ward sister and acquaint her with any habits your child may have (inability to sleep without the light on, etc.). Help the child to settle in a calm, friendly way. Avoid making hospital seem a child's idea of Eden, crammed with ice-cream, constant Lego and unlimited telly.

Once you have gone, the patient will get an inkling that everything in the garden isn't rosy when face and teeth have to be washed, and boxes of guzzly goodies are firmly removed by a nurse. He will wake to a breakfastless morning and may not feel at all sparkling for some time. Paint a pleasant but realistic picture so that he will understand what is happening and why.

During your visits to him, talk to him of what is happening at home, and when he feels like it, involve him in some activity, reading, games etc. On leaving, tell him exactly when he can expect to see you again. To a young child, vague indications that you'll be back soon are misleading, and can lead to confusion and even distress. It's a good idea to tell the child, "I'll come back tomorrow after breakfast", or, "I'll come again after lunch", and to appear when you say you will.

Many children will skip through a spell in hospital without a care in the world. However, it's worth bearing in mind that this fact may not emerge until after the event and that much can be done to help a sensitive child during this experience so that the effects of hospitalisation can be positive. You may find that your child has not only lost his tonsils but found some new friends!

STRESS

Some children are more resilient than others in reacting to and coping with stress. Apart from the disturbances caused by overwhelming stress (for instance, a parent's death), there are many stresses of a lesser nature which have to be absorbed as a normal part of a child's growth in his family. Many children seem able to overcome these stresses and achieve emotional maturity and stability. This ability is partly due to the fact that these children can communicate adequately. It is on the mastery of a reliable means of communication that the resilience of healthy childhood is based. It has been found that when they could communicate adequately, children in hospital (in residential care away from their families) and those who are handicapped, show this resilience.

The child who is unable to cope efficiently with the demands of the world at the moment, needs help so that this inability will be temporary and not remain a drawback. Children in this position tend to be uncertain of themselves in relationships and inhibited both in play and learning. They can find difficulty in making decisions and in recovering from crises. They cannot competently bear tension and cope with frustration. Sometimes a child's speech and behaviour can be disturbed as a result. Severe shock can also disturb his speech. Minor stresses can affect speech in the case of the child who is unable to cope. The pre-school child may revert to baby talk when a new baby arrives to absorb his mother's time and energy. A young child may begin to stammer when he first goes to school. Some children find it much harder than others to cope with the various minor stresses and strains which are part of normal living.

Hospitalisation is an experience from which he can benefit.

Part Two
Speech Problems in Young Children

5

Is He Slow In Talking?

5

Is He Slow In Talking?

EACH CHILD HAS his own age of speech readiness. Some children are speaking in clear phrases by two years of age while others of the same age are just starting to say their first words clearly. The pattern within normal limits is different and individual.

The varying rates at which speech and language develop may therefore pose a query for parents. 'How do I know if my child is developing speech at the normal rate?' Broadly speaking, if a child has passed through the various stages of crying, gurgling, babbling and is attempting to say words, then his language is developing along the right lines. If a child is not talking *at all* by the age of two, then it is a good idea to seek professional advice.

Some children are slow to talk. In some cases a mother will remark, 'Well, of course his father and grandfather didn't start to string words together until about three years of age'. The family history and pattern of speech in the home environment need to be taken into consideration. Some of the causes of delayed speech are, hearing loss, mental handicap, low intelligence, lack of motivation, emotional conflicts, shift of handedness, illness, emotional shock, neurological factors and bilingual conflicts.

HEARING LOSS

Any child who cannot adequately hear spoken language can be delayed in talking. The child whose vocal play was interrupted by hearing loss may not have had a period of babbling in his speech development. He may therefore have been deprived of listening to and practising speech.

MENTAL HANDICAP

A child whose mental age is found to be lower than his actual age will most probably have a delayed speech development. With the present practice of health service to check each baby's development at six months, it should be possible to discover the baby with special problems, physical and mental handicap, so that effective help can be given at an early stage.

LACK OF MOTIVATION

There are some young children who are lazy about talking just as there are those who take their time in learning to walk. If a child does not feel a need to talk, he simply won't bother. For instance, an older brother or sister may interpret his needs and speak for him, so that the child feels he doesn't have to speak to get what he wants. Another child may in fact roar to let his mother know he wants a drink or his teddy. If roars will work instead of talking, the child may well not bother with speech. Parents may not expect a verbal response from the child. For instance a mother can anticipate the child's need and without waiting for the child to speak, rush in with the object of the child's desire, perhaps keeping up a running commentary. 'Do you want a drink? Yes you do, here you are then, a lovely drink of milk in your nice red mug. Show me how clever you are and drink it all up for Mama'. While the use of language here is stimulating, there has been no incentive for the child to speak. His mother's flow of eloquence barely leaves him time to draw breath, let along utter.

EMOTIONAL CONFLICTS

Talking is a powerful way to express ideas and emotions. While the child is growing and developing his skills of language and articulation, his emotions are playing an important part in his life. As his language grows, he begins to realise that this language can express his feelings more effectively than temper tantrums, screaming, or gesture. The young child needs plenty of opportunity to express his emotions which he does through language and imaginative play. Using language and movement, he can release in make-believe games for instance, feelings of aggression which might otherwise remain locked inside creating tensions and frustrations.

The young child who has difficulty in expressing his feelings, who experiences emotional conflict or who is under stress, may have delayed speech development or may temporarily regress to an earlier level of development. Since language expresses the child's emotions, it is understandable that when there is emotional conflict, this will be manifested in his speech. An example given earlier is the young child of three or four years who feels jealous of his new baby brother or sister. He considers the newcomer as a rival for his mother's affection and attention. As a result, he becomes aggressive in the home situation. He may revert to using 'baby talk' and behave like a baby, wetting his pants and drinking from a baby's bottle. The child who is able to express his feelings through play and by talking about them to his parents will be able to release these feelings of tension and aggression. One little girl expressed her conflicting feelings to her mother and new baby brother with the words, 'Hello Mama, Bye-Bye baby!' It is when the child is unable or afraid to express his fears and jealousies that these feelings, in themselves normal reactions, may be intensified causing a build up of frustration and tension. One little boy started to say his first words when he was seventeen months old. For the next year or so, the family suffered major upheaval and strain, moving to another continent, separated often for reasons of work from the father, and living in a succession of temporary dwellings and tents. The child's speech progress seemed to halt to such an extent that his parents feared he might be deaf. The only words he used were 'Mama' and 'Dada' — his progress in the area of toilet training came to a similar halt. A happy relationship had always existed between this child and his baby brother and when the latter started to say his first words at the age of ten months, the older child (who was two-and-a-quarter years) adopted his brother's level of speech development and both boys progressed to having long conversations in jargon. At last the family situation was resolved and on the first evening in a 'proper' house, the child who by this time was two years and nine months spoke his first sentence: 'Mama, I want potty'. From that moment on, he resumed his developmental progress. He became toilet trained shortly afterwards and soon was way ahead of his young brother in terms of vocabulary and powers of expression.

WHICH HAND – LEFT OR RIGHT?

It has been found that a child's language may become confused if there is a shift of handedness or if a child has mixed handedness. Sometimes parents and teachers press a child to use his right hand when in fact the child is left-handed. The reason for the resulting confused language is a neurological one. Research[5] has shown that for most people the speech centre is on the left side of the brain. This centre lies close to the centre responsible for movement. It is known that the left side of the brain controls movements of the right side of the body and vice versa. The process by which the left side of the brain gains control over speech is a gradual one. We can see from this that if a child's handedness is confused, a resulting confusion in speech can occur. It is important therefore to ensure that a child gets plenty of opportunity to develop his tendency to be either right- or left-handed.

ILLNESS

Severe or prolonged illness during the first year of life can have the effect of interrupting the baby's babbling period and may affect his speech development. Prolonged illness or frequent bouts of illness in the young child may have the effect of shutting a child away from essential experience at a crucial time in his language growth. He may be delayed in talking as a result.

EMOTIONAL SHOCK

Occasionally a severe fright or other strong emotion can interrupt or halt the normal development of speech and language.

NEUROLOGICAL FACTORS

One of the more uncommon reasons for delayed speech is severe birth injury or injury after birth which may cause Aphasia or in it's less severe form, Dysphasia. The child who is aphasic has difficulty in understanding or expressing language, sometimes both. The Dysphasic child has the same difficulties to a lesser extent. This condition requires diagnosis and specialised treatment, especially speech therapy. There are some children who appear to have minimal brain damage and in these cases speech may be delayed.

PHYSICAL HANDICAP

Where a child is physically handicapped, he may be slow in developing language.

BILINGUAL PROBLEMS

The pre-school child in a bilingual environment may be delayed in developing speech and language particularly if his mother speaks in two languages to him. There are plenty of young children who experience no speech problems in being bilingual. However there is a tendency for the pre-school child to be confused if he is expected to use two languages. The older child of five, for example, who has been reared in one language, and then attends a school where another language is spoken, shouldn't show confusion in his speech, provided he has achieved mastery of the structure and forms of one language before he started school. It is important to realise however, that with the varying rates of speech and language development, not every five-year-old is ready for a second language.

If a child does not feel a need to talk he simply won't bother.

Guidelines

IS HE SLOW IN TALKING?

Seek professional advice if your child is not talking *at all* by the age of twenty-four months.

A child's speech progress can be interrupted or halted by illness and emotional conflicts etc.

Do not keep a child back from a playgroup or school just because he is not talking as well as his friends.

Make sure your child gets specialised help if he has a special problem.

Don't panic if your child is slow in talking. Many children are slow to start, but once they get going, nothing can stop them.

Is he right- or left-handed? Give him the chance to find out.

Keep pace with the child's level of speech development.

Seek professional advice if you are concerned about your child's speech.

6
He Doesn't Speak Clearly

Environmental Factors

Organic Defects

Emotional Conflicts

Motor In-coordination

Perceptual Difficulties

Songs and Rhymes

Sound Games

Guidelines at a Glance

6

He Doesn't
Speak Clearly

WHEN HE HAS learned to use words and short phrases, the child turns to the sophisticated business of speaking clearly so that what he says can be readily understood. This process has started long before the child's speech is intelligible. To speak clearly the child needs to make co-ordinated movements of the tongue, lips, jaw and soft palate. The baby listens to speech sounds and experiments with them during vocal play. He later learns the rhythms of words and that words have a beginning, middle and end. He learns to discriminate between sounds and to repeat sounds in sequence. When he hears words or sounds he is able to remember and reproduce them exactly as he heard them. He gradually becomes able to remember and reproduce more sounds or words at one time. For example, a mother says, 'Oh look at the cat', and the child says 'cat'. Later on, a mother could say, 'There's Goldilocks, sleeping in baby bear's bed', and the child would be able to remember and repeat exactly what her mother had said. The child learns to move his tongue, lips, jaws and soft palate. All this is practice for speech, as are his chewing and swallowing movements. He can get great fun as he becomes interested in sounds, in sorting them out and practising them in sound games.

The age at which he starts to talk in turn influences the length of time it will take before he is speaking clearly articulated sentences..

A child who speaks in phrases at two years and by three years is using sentences with a correct use of prepositions, pronouns and tenses, can be speaking clearly by the age of four. On the other hand, a child who started using phrases at three years, may be five before all that he says is readily understood.

The first sounds mastered are the vowels, then the lip sounds, B, P and M. Then the front and back tongue sounds, t, d, n, k, ng, g. Next the complicated sounds f, v, l, s, z, sh, ch, r, z (as in raj) and j (as in jam) and finally the blends gr, bl, sw, str and so on. The age at which they are mastered varies. Some children may master the sounds but take quite a long while to master S and R sounds.

The child who doesn't speak clearly may substitute a different sound for the correct one. For example 'tock' for 'clock' or 'tee-taw' for 'see-saw'. He may omit or distort a particular sound. He may omit the endings of words. His speech can sound confused and may even be unintelligible. The mistakes he makes in his speech sounds may be consistent so that for example he may always say 'thand' and 'thally' for 'sand' and 'Sally' or the pattern may be inconsistent and jumbled.

ENVIRONMENTAL FACTORS

If a parent has a speech defect or is deaf, the child may be influenced by these factors and may not speak clearly as a result. Faulty articulation can be caused by pressures exerted on the child while he is developing speech. Speech standards in the home that are too high, forcing the child to recite in public or mocking the child's way of speech, are a few examples of situations which put pressure on a child's speech.

A child may imitate the speech of an older playmate who 'lisps' for instance (to pronounce S and Z sounds incorrectly). The American speech pathologist, Charles Van Riper, has an interesting comment on this situation. 'It is said that S and Z are pronounced as 'th' in Castillian Spanish because a certain king of Spain 'lisped' and his courtiers adopted his pronunciation of the sibilant sounds. Little tyrants in every child kingdom similarly impose their speech peculiarities upon their subjects'.

ORGANIC DEFECTS

Severe or partial hearing loss should be detected as early as possible. Some children have a partial hearing loss which consists of a difficulty in hearing sounds in the high frequency range. Such a child may well have difficulty in pronouncing S, Sh, Ch, etc. He may even leave out these sounds from his speech. If a child has a cleft palate, this can cause faulty articulation. To have a cleft palate means that the child's palate is divided so that there is no longer a proper roof to the mouth and floor to the nose. This condition is discussed on page 134. In the case of a child with a tongue tie, this condition is less likely to cause difficulties than people generally think. Unless the tie is extremely tight, most children adapt to the situation. These conditions should be medically assessed as soon as they are discovered. Speakers may have protruding upper teeth, an excessively long tongue or an overshot jaw. These problems cannot be termed essential causes of faulty articulation, nevertheless they may certainly be an inhibiting factor in speech development. Persistent thumb sucking can alter the shape of the mouth and cause the upper teeth to protrude. Protruding upper teeth may need orthodontic treatment, which is indicated if your child has teeth which need to be moved because they are crooked, protruding, receding, spaced out and so on. Orthodontia is ideally done between the ages of eight and thirteen when the growth process of the child's teeth can be used to advantage.

EMOTIONAL CONFLICTS

There are some children who experience more difficulty than others in separating from their parents and forming relationships outside the home. There can be a number of reasons for this, ranging from over-protectiveness on the part of the parents, to a shy and retiring disposition on the part of the child. The child may hang back from reaching a mature level of speech and keep up a form of 'baby talk' or mispronounce his S and R sounds; 'woly poly' for 'roly poly', 'thwee thweeth' for 'three sweets'. The desire to remain a child, or return to childhood security can result in faulty articulation. This doesn't mean that a child who doesn't say his S sounds clearly is always immature. Indeed temporary slight hearing loss in the high frequency range could well be the cause.

MOTOR-IN-COORDINATION

If the child has difficulty in moving the muscles

used in speech then some faulty articulation can be expected. In the case of the spastic child who has difficulty in moving his muscles, a similar difficulty can affect his speech muscles.

PERCEPTUAL DIFFICULTIES

Some children can hear speech but they may have difficulty in 'attending to' the sounds of speech, in discriminating between sounds, and in realising where sounds occur in words. They may have a jumbled idea of the number of syllables in a word, of the sequence of the syllables and usually have difficulty in repeating sounds, syllables and words in sequence. A child with this type of difficulty can confuse syllables in words and say for example, 'chingel' for 'children' or 'bakset' for 'basket'. This sort of pronunciation is quite acceptable in the pre-school child who is still developing language and needs no treatment. However, in a child of seven or eight years old, articulation of this sort should be investigated.

You can play simple games with your child to promote skills of articulation provided they are undertaken as *games* and not exercises. Rhyming and guessing games are great fun for the young child who is fascinated by them and often makes up his own versions.

If your child is not speaking clearly by the time he starts school, contact his teacher. If possible, the teacher should try to understand the child's speech without asking him to repeat what he has said. It may be necessary for parents and teacher to discuss this because what is easily understood by the child's family may in fact sound quite unintelligible to the teacher. The help the child needs at this stage consists of (a) sound and listening games (perhaps Montessori sound boxes); (b) general articulation games, provided they are played with other children as speech games, and not as a corrective measure; (c) more defined listening games. I have already given a few suggestions for speech games. I must stress that these are not a prerequisite for clarity of speech but rather guidelines to follow which, while being fun, may also *unobtrusively* encourage the child's speech skills. Bear in mind when inventing games of this sort that the child's concentration is apt to stray after a few minutes so have plenty of variety. Movement associated with sound is more effective than rhymes or sound games on their own.

SONGS AND RHYMES

The origin of some of these songs escapes me. You may be familiar with some or all of them.

1. Marching songs — in time to music: 1, 2, 1, 2 march, march, 1, 2.

2. Clapping in time to familiar rhymes like:
   Baba Black Sheep, Little Bo-Peep.

3. Hopping Rhymes —
   Hoppity Hop, Hoppity Hop
   I'm on my way, and I cannot stop,
   Hoppity Hop, etc.

4. Ding-Dong-Ding-Dong
   Ring the Bell!
   Ding-Dong-Ding-Dong
   Ring it well

5. Bang, Bang, Bang
   I play on my drum
   Bang, Bang, Bang,
   Rumpity-Tumpity-Tum

6. I hear a bee mmm
   I hear a clock tick tock
   I hear a bell ding dong
   Keep them all going
   Don't let them stop
   Mmm, tick-tock, ding-dong.

7. I have a little bicycle
   I got it at the shop
   And when I see the big red lights
   I know I have to stop

SOUND GAMES

1. Arrange some toy animals in a 'farmhouse'. Ask the child to move an animal into the 'field' or 'farmyard' when he hears you making that particular animal's sound, e.g. miaou for cat.

2. Select some speech sounds and associate them with activities. Ask the child to do the action corresponding to the sound he hears. Mmm (driving a car), SH — the sound of rushing wind (said as a vocal glide), for an aeroplane AHHhha, PUH — drops of rain etc.

3. Give three or four children a special sound each. Explain that the sounds are going to have a race across the room. Ask each child to step forward once when you make his particular sound, e.g. k-k (gun noise), Ch,Ch,Ch, (Train); SSS (hissing snake) etc.

4. Another version of the last game (3) can be played with one child who moves toys when he hears their particular sounds.

5. Individual speech sounds can be practised by associating them with activities: SH — wind sound. It's better to stick to *one* association for each sound as otherwise the child may become confused.

6. Nonsense sounds can also be used in games, since the child is being helped to *listen* and differentiate between sounds.

7. Place five things which start with the same sound on a table or in a box. Allow the child to select random items and say them for him so that he can listen for the sound at the beginning of the word.

8. Games played with cards containing pictures of like sounding words: hat, man, mat, sand, can, pan. Say one word, ask the child to indicate the object you name. Then name all of the objects while the child indicates them. Do not correct him if he is wrong.

He may revert to using baby talk.

Guidelines

HE DOESN'T SPEAK CLEARLY

Seek professional advice if in doubt about your child's articulation.

Do not correct your child's faulty articulation.

Seek the advice of your dentist if your child has crooked or protruding teeth.

Make sure the school-going child's faulty articulation is not corrected in class.

Play general listening games and sound games with the child.

Use songs and rhymes to help his sense of rhythm and speech.

Watch out for any recurring ear, nose or throat problems.

Seek help if you suspect any hearing loss in your child.

7
Voices

7
Voices

VOICE REFLECTS personality and background. There are as many voices as there are personalities. Voice tone can carry hostility, aggression, gentleness, timidity. A particular type of voice can run in a family — a deep throaty voice, or in contrast, a highly pitched nervous voice. A person's voice exists in relation to his local, social and cultural surroundings and should be accepted as part and parcel of that person. In some areas where a nasal voice is part of the local accent, it should be accepted as such. Like many other things we use all the time, the voice is apt to be taken for granted. Here is a very brief description of the human voice, as given by Gwynneth Thurburn[6].

"To make any sound three things are necessary:

An Excitor
A Vibrator
A Resonator

In the human voice, the breath is the force, the vocal cords comprise the vibrator, and the mouth, neck and nose the resonating cavities. A quantity of air is expelled from the lungs and passes between the edges of the vocal cords, causing them to vibrate. These vibrations pass through the hollow spaces of the neck and mouth where they are amplified in the same way that sound passing through a megaphone is increased and changed. (The nose and hollow spaces in the bones of the face act as accessory resonators.''). The voice of a young child is high compared to that of an adult. In puberty, major pitch changes occur. A boy's voice drops usually an octave and at the upper end of the pitch range, there is a slight but noticeable loss. A girl's voice drops from one to three tones and there is an equivalent gain at the upper end of the pitch range. These pitch changes occur because in puberty the vocal cords grow one third of their length in about six months.

LOSS OF VOICE

It may happen that a child can suddenly lose his voice. Where this is not caused by anything physical, the reason may be an emotional shock. Specialist investigation is needed in such rare cases.

HOARSENESS

One of the commonest reasons for hoarseness in children is shouting. Shouting in the playground and at football games are instances of areas where the 'playground voice' develops. Persistent hoarseness and constantly recurring sore throats and difficulty in swallowing need ear, nose and throat investigation.

HEARING LOSS

The child with hearing loss may speak too loudly and also may have a voice which sounds monotonous as he has difficulty in hearing the cadences, rhythms and inflections of normal speech. The child with the special problem of hearing loss is discussed on page 115.

VOICE TONE

Voice tone may lack inflection and intonation or contain too much or too little nasality. The child with a cleft palate usually speaks with too much nasality. Since his palate, which acts as a roof to the mouth and a floor to the nose, is not functioning adequately, breath used for speaking tends to 'leak' up into the nose causing the voice tone to be nasalised. Some children have a cleft palate type speech even though the soft palate is intact. This can occur if the soft palate is too short to shut off the mouth from the nose.

MUFFLED VOICE

The child with enlarged tonsils and adenoids may have a voice which sounds muffled as a result of these conditions. As these can often be associated with ear conditions, the child's hearing may be slightly affected temporarily. If this occurs often, the child will have to strain to hear what is said and the effort involved tends to sap his energies which can already be below par. He is in a state of uncertainty, not being sure that he has correctly caught the exact meaning of what is said to him. He may also shout in conversational speech and be heedless when spoken to. Often parents unwittingly label such children dull or cantankerous.

The best treatment for all constantly recurring

ear, nose and throat problems is to seek the advice of a specialist. Keep a check on these problems as they occur since neglect may have adverse results on voice, speech, and hearing. If a child shows persistent signs of a 'stuffy' nose or suffers from chronic nasal discharge, or if his voice sounds muffled over long periods, these conditions should be investigated. The hoarse ardent football fan who can't enjoy a match unless he lustily yells his support, should be encouraged to obtain a 'clacker' or noise maker which he can use with gusto to give his team the loud support they need without straining his voice.

The child whose voice lacks intensity may be a shy and retiring person. As long as it is audible, this type of voice is perfectly acceptable unless it is a cause of embarrassment to the *child*. Quite often parents set the standards for the voice they wish their child to have and feel disappointed when the child does not fulfil their expectations.

They can express their feelings through voice.

Guidelines

VOICES

Seek medical advice if your child has recurring ear, nose or throat problems such as muffled voice, 'stuffy nose', 'runny ears', laryngitis.

Remember that voice expresses personality and that your child's voice will be influenced by the social and cultural factors in his environment.

Seek help if you suspect hearing loss in your child.

8
Stammering

8

Stammering

STAMMERING IS A complex problem. It interferes with communication and is often associated with distress and anxiety on the part of the person who stammers, and a feeling of rejection and embarrassment on the part of the listeners. The terms stammering and stuttering are synonymous. British and American figures give the incidence of stammering as one percent of the population, and two percent to four percent in school children. On the basis of British and American figures there could well be ten thousand stammerers in a small country the size of Ireland.

DEFINITION

Stammering is a speech disorder in which interruptions of the flow of speech occur. These may take the form of repetitions, blocks or prolongations of which the stammerer may be unaware. On the other hand, the hesitations and prolongations may occur so often that he realises they interfere with his communication. He then reacts by struggling and later may avoid talking whenever possible. He devises tricks to start a word or to interrupt or postpone talking. His fear of talking makes the stammer worse. A person with this type of stammer often has many ways of starting, avoiding, postponing and releasing speech when blocks occur. Stammering most often starts in childhood between the ages of three and five when the child is mastering his fluency skills, although it is not uncommon for the onset of the stammer to occur at seven years or in adolescence. More boys than girls stammer and it can run in families and can be aggravated by stress and pressures in the environment.

There is no single known cause of stammering and no certain cure. The onset can be drastic and may be associated with shock or emotional conflicts. More frequently it starts so gradually that parents find it difficult to state the date with any certainty. Stammering is caused by many factors. A child's co-ordination may be poor, he may become easily frustrated or he may come from a background where there is emotional conflict. Other factors could be a speech environment which hinders fluency, or stress, suffered by the child who is pushed into speaking in sentences before he is able. The last factor is probably the most common cause.

PRIMARY STAMMERING

Where the child's speech is less fluent than normal with very frequent repetitions and prolongations, he is stammering. In primary stammering he is not aware of these hesitations and does not struggle with or fear them. It is important to realise that there is a difference between a stage of non-fluency and actual stammering. Research indicates that while the non-stammerer shows most of his hesitancy in completing his thought, the stammerer has difficulty in *speaking* his thoughts to people. The young child who stammers without being aware of it, may nonetheless be aware that others are embarrassed by his way of talking. As some children mature, there is a gradual disappearance of the primary stammer. As a child grows and develops so do his skills and contacts with his surroundings. At first this may be confusing for him and he may start to stammer, but as he continues to develop he learns to cope with excitement and a certain amount of tension in his environment. As he becomes more stable, the stammer often disappears. But this only happens if he has not been aware of it as a handicap. *If he can be prevented from reacting to his stammer, he will not develop a whole series of devices to start, postpone, avoid and release speech when blocks occur. His stammer will not become a habit and he is not likely to become anxious about his speech.* In cases of primary stammering, treatment is aimed at maintaining a lack of awareness and anxiety, towards removing factors which disturb smoothness of speech. It helps to provide experiences of fluency and to strengthen the child's resistance to the pressures which aggravate the stammer.

If a child is stammering, it is important to prevent him from reacting to his stammer. It is also important to prevent him becoming anxious about the way he speaks. By all means seek advice and remember that attitudes on the part of those in the child's environment play a vital part. Accept the fact that he is stammering as his way of speaking at present. If the reaction to the child's speech is surprise, embarrassment or anxiety, he will be aware that there is something wrong with the way he talks and will react likewise. Talk simply to the child who stammers, using short sentences, so that he doesn't feel pressed to achieve a standard which is beyond him. Ensure that there is time to listen. Listen to *what* the child says: not to how he speaks. A pleasant home environment, where his stammer is accepted as his current mode of expression, and where there is no undue tension, can help the child enormously. Stress and pressures should be reduced. There are many stresses in everyday life, and they have to be absorbed by the child as a normal part of his growth. It is unrealistic to expect an environment to be without tension and we all have to learn to cope with a certain degree of it. This is quite healthy and useful. Some children are more resilient than others when coping with stress so that what amounts to a pressure in the case of one child, may not bother another. It is difficult therefore to generalise.

Some of the following situations can make a child feel he is under pressure. Forcing and nagging a child to learn ballet or music and to be better at sports or lessons, can have the undesired effect of making the child feel he's in a race that he must win. Placing undue emphasis on speech by urging the child to speak slowly, take a deep breath, or speak as clearly as his sister, can place too much pressure on the child. Correcting or interrupting the child while he is talking can make matters worse.

Parental anxiety is quite easily sensed by a child. It is important to distinguish between parental anxiety, and parental concern about the child's speech. If a parent is anxious when his child stammers the tendency is to panic and feel unable to change the child's stammer. This can result in frustration and perhaps feelings of guilt. The important point is that parental concern for the child's speech progress is quite healthy and constructive and need not lead to anxiety and over concern. In my opinion, few parents are aware of the power they possess to *help* a child who stammers. This is possibly due to adverse social reactions to stammering — viewing it as a handicap, and a general lack of awareness and understanding of the problem. Parents should ensure that the child gets as much rest and relaxation as he needs. Tension, which has been found to be a precipitating cause of stammering, can build up when a child's strength and health are over-taxed. Indeed, speech situations which encourage fluency can be created at home. Encourage the child to tell you stories and to recite *when he is willing* and in the absence of pressure. This does not mean reciting in public or in front of relatives. Build up his self-confidence in other areas such as music, painting, reading and dancing *if* he shows an interest in them. It is important to use these activities to promote his self-confidence and not as a basis for competition with his brothers and sisters or classmates. Parents and teachers can cancel any unpleasant memories and experiences associated with stammering by distracting the child's attention following a stammer. This should be done as effortlessly as possible.

If your child stammers and is a twin, it can sometimes be a help if each twin is in a different class at school so that the twin who stammers is not eclipsed by the other and is given every chance to progress at his own rate and exist as a person in his own right and not as one of a pair.

Fluent speech requires, among other factors, intricate timing of muscular co-ordinations. There are some children who are awkward just as there are those who are very well co-ordinated. Some children are awkward at speaking and can get tangled up in speech, and have more hesitations, than those who are 'fleet of tongue'. This may well be a contributing factor to the origin of stammering.

The young child who is not allowed to establish his laterality and who is forced, perhaps unwittingly, to use his right hand when in fact he is left-handed, may, as a result of this confusion, develop a stammer. This is one of the reasons why it is essential to allow a child's natural laterality to establish itself.

At school, the child's teacher can help the child who stammers. A young child with a primary stammer can be prevented from reacting to it at school as well as at home. An understanding teacher can create an attitude of acceptance, so that other children do not react emotionally to the child who stammers. She can cancel any unpleasant memories or experiences of stammering by distracting the child immediately after he stammers. She can help the child to establish his handedness if this is needed. She can also encourage the child to recite, tell stories and talk about his interests when he is willing. Teachers should see that no undue emphasis is placed on the child's speech and make sure that he is *not* told to 'take a deep breath' or 'go slowly'. By ignoring the primary stammer, the teacher can help the child and also sets an example for his class-mates to follow. She can also ensure that the child is not mocked or teased because of his speech.

One teacher used the following method to prevent a class from teasing a stammerer. When the child was absent from school, she gathered the children together and told them that just as each child could do something like painting, or arithmetic better than other children, so you also found that everyone was not able to be the best at everything. 'Mary, you're so good at adding while John is great at speech'. She then went on to mention that the absent child was very good at painting and explained that everyone was different which made life more interesting. Then she mentioned how important it was to remember this and *not to tease* anyone who didn't seem to be good at a particular thing like adding or speech. One of the children said that the absent child kept repeating his words all the time. To this the teacher replied that their classmate did have a little difficulty with his speech at the moment, but that he would get over it sooner if everyone gave him plenty of time and did not pay any attention to the differences in his speech. The part played by the teacher in this instance was invaluable and helped enormously to prevent that particular child from developing a secondary stammer.

Guidelines

PRIMARY STAMMERING

Seek professional advice.

Accept a period of non-fluency as normal and do not confuse it with stammering. (Seek advice about this if in doubt).

Do not place undue emphasis on your child's speech or make him aware of his stammer.

Remember that anxiety does not help and can, in fact, hinder his speech fluency.

Listen to *what* the child says, not how he speaks.

Do not rush, correct or interrupt the child while he is talking.

Do not discuss your child's stammer in his presence as if he weren't in the room.

Do not set too high a standard of speech for him to follow.

Do not use remarks such as, 'Take a deep breath' or 'Slow down'.

Reduce pressures in the environment. Remember that a child may stammer when under stress.

Allow the child to establish his laterality (handedness) if he hasn't already done so.

Give realistic standards of fluency for your child to follow by speaking in short, simple sentences.

Make time to listen to what he has to say.

Do not supply a 'missing word' for the child when he stammers.

Do contact the child's teacher and put her in the picture.

Ensure the child is not teased or mocked.

Do not allow other children to speak for him or to interrupt or correct his speech.

Build up his self-confidence by promoting his interest in activities (swimming, music, clubs etc.). Give him the same degree of responsibility (according to his age) at home as you do the others in the family.

Remember that as parents, teachers and interested adults in the child's environment, you can *help* to prevent the child from reacting adversely to a primary stammer.

SECONDARY STAMMERING

When a child is aware that he stammers and is anxious about it, the stammering can become a habit. As he redoubles his efforts to speak or tries to control his speech by forcing out the word he wants to say or by substituting another, he may become tired and frustrated. He may blink his eyes, nod his head or stamp his foot as part of the struggle to speak, and can become embarassed and even distressed about his speech. The major difference between primary and secondary stammering is that in secondary stammering the speaker is conscious of the fact that he stammers and reacts emotionally to it. Once these symptoms have been established, the child is not only aware that he stammers but anxious as well.

Since each case is individual, treatment varies, and no specific set of 'instructions' are available. Treatment may well include some of the methods used in cases of primary stammering. Added to this, the child with a secondary stammer needs treatment which is aimed at preventing the stammer from becoming a habit. Treatment should also be aimed at reducing underlying tensions. The child who stammers should be gradually led to the stage where he can explore and evaluate his attitude towards his speech and learn to modify and control his stammer. He will be more likely to give up such tactics as avoiding to talk when he realises they are barriers to fluent speech. Treatment should help him to cope with his fear of speaking and attempt to reduce the amount of fear present. Everything should be done to promote his self-confidence. Since the child who stammers exists in relation to his environment, it is impossible to treat the stammerer without the co-operation of those around him and without attempting to reduce or eliminate pressures which are aggravating the problem.

For example, too high a standard may be demanded of the child either in school or socially. Sometimes children are encouraged to take part in competitive music or drama activities, and forced to perform in public, or to take on responsibilities at home for which they are not sufficiently mature. These and other such situations can cause tension. Positive help can be given in school to the child who stammers. One of the most important things a teacher can do is to show by her *attitude* that she understands and accepts the child's way of speaking. This means allowing the child time to talk, without correction or interruption. Reactions of impatience, embarassment, pity or rejection only tend to reinforce the stammerer's lack of confidence in his speech and make him more aware that his method of talking is different.

The school-going child who has a secondary stammer needs to be referred to a speech therapist. He can be significantly helped in the class room by the teacher who can find ways to increase his self-confidence. Since stammering is a complex problem, there can be no set of instructions to be applied generally. Treatment is tailored to the needs of the individual. Close contact is essential between the teacher and speech therapist. Bear in mind that if the child is under stress or emotionally disturbed, he may stammer. The teacher can reduce the stammerer's feelings of tension and frustration by creating outlets for his emotional expressions, for example, through drama.

The child who stammers should not be forced

to speak or read in class but neither should he be passed over. This clearly presents a problem. 'I never know whether to ask him to read aloud or not', is a frequent remark made by teachers who are eager to help the secondary stammerer, and understandably confused by the vast amount of conflicting theories and methods of treatment for stammering. Children usually do not like to be singled out in class by being ignored when the others take their turn to read aloud.

Where possible, the teacher should discuss the child's speech difficulty with him. This can be done objectively when teacher and child are alone. This will let the teacher know the extent of the child's fear and avoidance of speaking in class (e.g. whether the child prefers to read aloud or not) and show the child that the teacher realises he has a speech problem and wishes to help him in a practical way.

Asking the class to read aloud in pairs can be a help to the secondary stammerer. The child should not be forced into a speaking situation but neither should he be ignored or simply passed over. I consider there is nothing to be gained from the practice of standing up in class to recite knowledge learned by heart. It can cause fear and tension and does not ensure that children *learn*. Moreover, for the child who stammers, it could mean the removal of one cause of tension in the environment. There is however a need for children to speak in front of others and this should be, encouraged on a voluntary basis so that each child views public speaking in a positive light. Drama can be used as a means to help the child who stammers, as a supplement to treatment. Small groups can be arranged for debates or mock television interviews or job interviews in the case of older children. Informal discussions help to provide opportunities for the child to speak voluntarily and without pressure.

The attitude and reaction of listeners to the child who stammers are extremely important. The stammerer can usually read fluently when alone. His difficulty is not in speaking but in *speaking to people.* Sadly, people often mock or pity the stammerer because of their own lack of understanding. Of course, a certain amount of teasing takes place among playmates and everyone has to learn to live with this, including the child who stammers. But he should not be subjected to cruel taunts and unnecessary reactions to the way he speaks.

ATTITUDE OF SOCIETY TO THE STAMMERER

The many origins of stammering and the host of varying theories have undoubtedly added to general confusion on the subject. The attitude and reaction of society to the stammerer can help or hinder him. Quite a number of people think children may be 'putting on' a stammer or that it is helpful to the child to correct him. Most of the adverse reactions of society to the stammer as previously stated, exist because of a lack of awareness and understanding of the problem. It should not be accepted that teasing, mocking or rejecting the stammerer is normal. After all, is the mocking of physical handicaps accepted as a normal reaction? A stammerer can, with help, learn to view his situation with insight and a sense of humour. He can learn to cope with and change his speech. He needs help both professionally and in his daily life. We, as parents, teachers, employers and general members of the public can help by our understanding and consideration.

The child needs time to think of what to say,
and time to say it.

Guidelines

Seek professional advice.

Contact your child's teacher so that he or she can help.

Build up your child's self-confidence.

Remove and eliminate pressures.

Ensure the child gets adequate rest and relaxation.

Try to accept the way the child talks without anxiety or embarassment.

Do not correct his speech, interrupt or supply a missing word for him.

Do not demand standards that are too high in speech, sports, arts or academic work.

Create opportunities to discuss the child's speech with him in private if he wishes.

Since stammering problems are related to the child's environment, co-operation is needed on the part of the school, home, speech clinic, to ensure that treatment and understanding are carried over to all parts of his daily life.

Do not say, 'take a deep breath'. Breathing exercises, which can be an aid to relaxation achieve nothing unless underlying tensions are investigated and minimised.

9
Deafness

9
Deafness

THERE ARE VARIOUS types of deafness, the severity or the degree of hearing loss varies from the profoundly deaf child to the child with only partial hearing loss. Total deafness, that is, the inability to hear any sound, is extremely rare, perhaps non-existent in the child who is born deaf. There is usually some residual hearing even in the child who is born deaf, which must be utilised to *maximum* advantage at the earliest possible stage so that the child is not isolated in a silent world.

As noted earlier, sounds are received and transferred by our ears, and the message is then carried up to our brains. The outer ear collects the sounds and transmits them to the middle ear where the vibrations of the ear drum are transmitted to the inner ear. Sounds arrive as pressure waves in the air and are changed in the ear into electrical waves which are carried by nerve pathways to the brain.

CAUSES OF DEAFNESS

Deafness can occur if there is disease or injury to any part of the hearing apparatus from the outer ear to the brain. In conductive deafness, for example, disease of the outer or middle ear interferes with the passage of sound waves to the inner ear. In perceptive or nerve deafness, the nerve pathways are damaged and unable to adequately carry messages to the brain. Deafness may be a mixture of conductive and perceptive deafness. In rare cases, the sounds are carried normally to the brain but here the actual interpretation of sounds is impaired. This is called central deafness and is associated with a generalised disorder of the central nervous system, one of the symptoms of which is mental backwardness.

Deafness can be inherited. It can be caused by a disease, such as German measles during the early stages of pregnancy. It can also be caused by deformities of the outer or middle ear. A child may be born deaf or become deaf later. Some of the causes of acquired deafness are: inflammation of the middle ear (acute or chronic otitis media), injury or infections due to viruses and bacteria such as inflammation of the brain (encephalitis), inflammation of the covering of the brain and spinal cord (meningitis). Simple causes of deafness such as wax in the ear or catarrh in the passage (eustachian tube) leading from the back of the throat to the middle ear should not be overlooked. *Any suspicion of deafness requires immediate attention.* It is possible to test the reactions of babies to sounds, and severely deaf babies can be fitted with hearing aids. In this way they will be exposed to all sounds and will be more likely to comprehend and express themselves normally as they will be making the most use of their residual hearing at the earliest possible stage. When a child is not discovered to be deaf until he is three or four years old, valuable time has been lost.

There are various degrees of deafness and the deaf or hard-of-hearing child needs to be diagnosed and helped as early as possible. Deaf children are not backward. They vary in intelligence like all children. A deaf child of average intelligence who starts auditory training early can usually learn to hold his own in a hearing environment. The child who is born deaf, or becomes deaf before he has had a chance to develop language, has not had the opportunity to *learn to hear*. He must be supplied with sounds which are loud enough and which he hears often enough at an early age in a hearing environment. He needs individual attention and needs to associate words with their meanings in a relaxed atmosphere. He needs to be motivated to learn to hear and to talk. The age at which a child becomes deaf matters considerably, since a child's speech development can be arrested. In the absence of speech training, a young child who becomes deaf can lose his speech once he no longer hears his own voice or the speech of others. The speed of the onset of deafness also affects the child. To the child who suddenly becomes deaf (e.g. through meningitis), the effect can be catastrophic. The shock is terrific and the child can be completely bewildered since he cannot hear his voice and fears others cannot either. If a child becomes deaf after he has acquired speech, the ability to discriminate between consonants may become difficult or impossible since consonants are largely high-pitched sounds. Speech sounds are distorted and the child must work hard to recognise the difference between them.

When there is a hearing loss of high tones, even if hearing for lower tones is good, there is a problem. Background noises which are mainly low toned, are heard by the child and may mask the higher tones. As well as affecting the child's language development, voice and articulation, deafness imposes a barrier to comprehension and, not surprisingly, isolates the child. A deaf child can show his tension and frustration by throwing tantrums. The child who is hard of hearing may also feel considerable emotional tension. Often, the hearing loss of the hard-of-hearing child is not obvious, and people may think him stupid and the child can seem insecure and fearful of making mistakes.

HEARING TESTS

Ideally, deafness in babies should be discovered during the first year of life. Any child of two who fails to understand speech or to talk could be deaf. Deafness is not always easy to discover. Sometimes the sounds the baby makes seem similar to those made by babies with normal hearing. In some cases parents may have been told 'not to worry' and that 'everything will be alright', yet if carefully controlled tests are not undertaken, some hearing problems remain undetected. Babies' reactions to sounds can be tested and simple speech tests can be used with the very young child. Deafness can be measured by an audiometer which tests different pitches. Each ear is tested separately. This method is only suitable when the child is old enough to co-operate and to understand simple instructions.

Teachers of the deaf are specially trained to help the deaf child and the child with a partial hearing loss. The child may be referred to a speech therapist, depending on the type of hearing loss and how it is affecting his language, voice, and speech. Close co-operation is essential between speech therapists and teachers of the deaf. Teachers of the deaf are trained to help the child directly and indirectly by counselling the child's family and giving advice on hearing aids, lipreading, etc.

HEARING AIDS

Hearing aids amplify speech sounds to make them loud enough for the child to detect. Babies and children can be fitted with hearing aids which should be light, robust and easily wearable. They can be fitted to one or both ears. Body aids have a wire connected to a microphone, an amplifying system, and small battery all contained in a case which can be worn in a pocket or harness on the body. Ear-level aids are worn behind the ear between the ear lobe and the skull. These aids are light and comfortable. Bone conduction aids may be needed by a child prior to an operation for ear deformities. Hearing aids must be professionally prescribed and expertly fitted. Home training is needed so that the child can get used to the aid by perhaps wearing it for short periods at first. A hearing aid alone is of little value. It must be part of the child's learning programme.

Numerous fallacies about hearing aids exist, including that they cannot be used on babies, that any aid is good enough, that hearing aids impede lipreading or that the child is too deaf to benefit from an aid. Hearing aids *can* be used on babies under thirty six months and sometimes under two years. Delay means wasting valuable time. Any aid is *not* good enough. The child must have the correct aid for him.

To help him acquire hearing and speech, the deaf child needs to be bathed in sound. This is not education but an essential preliminary which normal children acquire *before* starting school. The deaf child needs intensive auditory training. The teacher of the deaf can give specific parental guidelines. It is vital that parents help the child and the importance of this help cannot be under-estimated. Deaf babies tend to lose interest in making sounds since they cannot hear them properly. It is very important therefore that mothers talk to deaf babies, giving them a pattern of speech and encouraging them to persist in making sounds. Constant repetition of words and phrases in association with meanings should be used by parents rather than isolated speech sounds. Speaking slowly in clear sentences, and with the normal rhythm of speech can help the deaf child. The young deaf child will also be helped if he can see the speaker's face, preferably at the same level as his own. Parents may be advised to speak direct-ly into the child's ear.

The work for parents of deaf children is enormous and at times seems frustrating and even hopeless. Many parents have felt an initial sense of hopelessness but have eventually had the satis-faction of seeing their child hold his own among hearing children. Support for parents is available from teachers of the deaf, audiologists and associa-tions for the deaf. The parents of the deaf child can be guided by those working with him as to the best way to help the child to become used to his hearing aid, and also to learn lip reading. When a child suddenly becomes deaf, lipreading should be started immediately, even if he is in hospital.

The sessions will be brief to start with. If a child is very young and only beginning to develop language when he becomes deaf, lipreading is even more essential since he may in the confusion, trauma and bewilderment, following deafness, forget the speech and language he has already acquired. A child can easily become withdrawn once the stimulus of conversation is missing.

LIPREADING

Lipreading has been called educated guesswork. Proficiency is dependent on sight, mental quickness and interest in people. It is not essential that hearing be 100% for lipreading to be successful. If the child grasps the key words or sufficient parts of key words, he may be able to fill in the rest in the same way as we can grasp the gist of a foreign language even though we only know a small percentage of the vocabulary. During lipreading practice, whole words or sentences can be spoken to the deaf child to be lipread as a whole, or he can learn what specific vowels and consonants look like individually. Whole words and sentences are usually used with children. As he gains confidence, a child needs to practise with other people.

EDUCATION

Deafness alone or deafness in combination with one or all of the associated disabilities of blindness, brain damage and emotional disturbance will need varying forms of education and care.

It is generally accepted that a child with a handicap benefits from living in a hearing community. Deaf children need to be educated to live in a normal hearing world and for this reason should not be segregated or placed in a protected environment except in some cases. There is also a need for special schools for the deaf which are geared to cope effectively and progressively with the problems of the profoundly deaf and severely hard of hearing. Since faulty methods of teaching the deaf are very difficult to erase, it is imperative that the child starts on the right road. Where possible the deaf child should be educated at a normal school; he needs to mix with hearing children. When deafness is not diagnosed until three or four years, the child can be retarded in general learning. He may seem dull or even disturbed. He should not be pushed into school before he has had a chance to make up for the lost years of listening. Attending a playgroup or nursery school where children talk loudly and simply can be helpful. A good unit catering for the partially deaf in a normal school can be a stepping stone for the deaf child.

Let the child see your face as you talk clearly
and simply, at a rate slower than normal
conversational speech.

Guidelines

THE DEAF CHILD

Seek help as soon as you suspect deafness.

Do not shout at the deaf child.

Show visitors how best to talk to your child.

Play *language* games with your child.

Let the child see your face, as you talk clearly and simply, at a rate that is slower than quick conversational speech.

Make sure he is motivated so that he will *want* to talk.

He should mix with hearing children of his own age.

10
Children With Special Problems

10

Children With Special Problems

IN THE PAST children with special problems tended to be rejected or pitied. Many remained isolated, their problems unresolved because of a general lack of awareness and understanding, and a lack of specialist help. To-day there are many associations for both parents and friends of children with special problems. I have given some addresses at the end of this book. There are also day centres and schools specifically organised to cope with special problems. If you are the parent of a child with a special problem such as hearing loss or mental handicap, remember you are not alone. It is vital to get the help needed for your child. Do not settle for second best, relying on the 'odd few hints' picked up from people you meet. There is a need for realistic goals, rather than overprotection and pity. Many children with special problems have associated speech defects. Let us look briefly at some of these conditions.

CEREBRAL PALSY

'Cerebral palsy is a condition causing partial paralysis in children. It may be due to disturbance of the normal development of the brain before birth, to injury during birth, or to illnesses or injury in early life. Because of their inability to move properly these children do not make the progress we take for granted in normal children. Their speech is often affected. Many of these children have normal intelligence and respond to treatment. This consists of teaching a new way of moving, to compensate for the lack of normal muscular control. For the person with cerebral palsy, the most ordinary activities are highly skilled accomplishments which must be acquired slowly and practised constantly. With proper training, begun early, suitable cases can go to ordinary schools, and follow ordinary careers afterwards; others need special schools, and probably protected occupations. In almost all cases, it is possible to make the victims of cerebral palsy less dependent on others for their care, whether at home or in institutions" *N.A.C.P. Ireland.*

There are various types of cerebral palsy, the most common being the spastic type and the athetoid types. The child who is spastic is stiff. His tendon jerks are exaggerated, and he has *too much* muscle tone but insufficient movement whereas the athetoid child has too much movement. The latter has difficulty in carrying out voluntary movements, for instance, he may wish to put his hand to his mouth but in doing so, causes awkwardness, and often the movement loses its direction completely.

50% — 70% of children with cerebral palsy have associated speech defects. This is according to the findings of the founder of the Bobath method for teaching new methods of movement to cerebral palsied children. Diagnosis of the child with cerebral palsy is difficult because of the widely differing degrees of severity, the varying types of cerebral palsy, the normal variations in the development of babies and the delayed appearance of signs of cerebral palsy.

At the present time, with regular assessment, children with cerebral palsy can usually be discovered within the first few years of life, usually by the age of three.

If a child has cerebral palsy he should be medically assessed and referred for treatment. Physiotherapy plays a major part in treatment and the physiotherapist will give you guidelines to follow and explain the stages of treatment. The child with cerebral palsy may have a speech defect. The aims of speech therapy will be to establish and maintain useful speech and intelligible communication. Before we can expect a spastic child to be readily understood when he talks, we must ensure that he can communicate verbally and use speech to express his needs. The extent to which he can do this will depend on many factors and progress takes time and patience on the part of the child, his parents, teachers and therapists.

The child with cerebral palsy may dribble, tend to keep his mouth open, be distractible and have limited tongue movements. He may have associated handicaps of hearing loss, mental handicap or dental defects. He may need to be referred for dental, ear, nose and throat, as well as psychological assessment. His associated handicaps need specialised treatment, and close co-operation between all those working on behalf of and with the child is not only advisable, but essential. Some specific problems related to speech handicap in the child can be minimised significantly with treatment. Much can be done at home to promote and sustain progress. Each child will have his own particular needs and rate of progress.

One of the most important aims is to make the child as independent as possible. By helping him to establish feeding and swallowing patterns and by eliminating drooling, you are in fact also helping his speech, since speech, breathing and feeding are all linked. The specialist team working with your child can give you precise information regarding the stages of treatment as they occur and specific guidelines to follow at each stage. You may be asked to make sure the child is sitting up, not lying back in the 'baby bird position' at meal-times. Placing small pieces of solid food at first into the child's mouth while you massage his cheeks will help him to chew. Also stroking his neck with downward stroking movements can help him to swallow the food. You may be asked to encourage the child to drink all cold drinks through a straw and to ensure he practises keeping his lips closed for short periods at a time (to help prevent dribbling). You can do this by placing a piece of paper between the child's lips and encouraging him to keep it there while you count up to five. Sucking, chewing and swallowing exercises may be used to help speech and prevent dribbling. Breathing exercises may be used both by physiotherapists and speech therapists.

A great obstacle to treatment of speech defects in spastic children is the uncontrolled spasmodic forward thrust of the tongue. When a child is over-excited these symptoms can be more pronounced so it is important to maintain a calm, relaxed approach in order to minimise muscular spasm. Mealtimes are especially important. It can take a bit of organisation on the part of parents but it is well worth it for the child. As far as possible, the child should be encouraged to eat with the family, as a member of the family group — this means eating the same menu and using the same utensils. He may need to have his food mashed at first, later loosely mashed, and then be introduced to solids. He should be encouraged to bite with his front teeth and chew with his back teeth. Scraping a metal spoon against the teeth can cause spasm. Special thick plastic straws can be of help for meals and exercises although it must be remembered that the aim of all treatment is to help the child towards independence which means, among other things, being able to eat meals anywhere with metal cutlery. A most important part of his independence means being able to communicate with others to the best of his ability.

CLEFT PALATE

A cleft palate means that there is an actual cleft or gap in the roof of the mouth or palate. Although some cleft palates are caused by accidents or injuries after birth, the majority occur during foetal life. 'During the sixth week of the unborn child's existence the primitive structures of the upper jaw grow very swiftly towards the midline and join those of the nose. This union is practically complete by the ninth week. This is what happens in most unborn children. But in a few, for reasons we do not entirely know, the timetable has been upset. The two shelves stop growing before they meet'. *Charles Van Riper.*

Cleft palate has occurred since earliest times. Smith and Dawson in their work 'Egyptian

Mummies' noted the discovery of one cleft palate. There are many variations of cleft palate. In some cases, the cleft may be hidden under the lining of the roof of the mouth and may be not more than a tiny perforation. More often the clefts are obvious ones. The cleft can be in (a) the movable soft palate; (b) in the hard and soft palates; (c) in both hard and soft palates as well as unilateral clefts in the upper gum and upper lip; (d) in both hard and soft palates and bilateral clefts in the upper gum and upper lip.

A cleft palate condition interferes with the functions of eating and speaking. Milk runs out of the nose; swallowing is interfered with; great quantities of air are taken in with tiny droplets of milk. If the upper lip is divided, the nipple cannot be grasped; a divided upper gum cannot press it. Feeding the baby who has a cleft palate is not an easy process. When the teeth appear, they can be misplaced and chewing can be poorly co-ordinated.

Cleft palate speech can be excessively nasal in tone and contain faulty articulation. The palate acts as a floor for the nose, and roof for the mouth; when it has a cleft or hole in it, the mouth and nose function differently in resonating sounds than they do when the palate is intact. Air leaks through the cleft into the nose instead of being directed out through the mouth. The voice can sound husky and breathy. Voice tone can resonate with too much nasality. Speech sounds can be distorted or even omitted. There is little evidence of operative work on cleft palates before the nineteenth century. Cleft palate surgery is among the most intricate ever to be mastered by man.

Surgery for closing palatal clefts is usually postponed until a child is from four to seven years of age. Children with cleft palates and cleft lips can have their first operation in the first year of life. Further surgery may be required when the child is three or four years old. Depending on the type of cleft, various operative techniques are used. The holes must be closed, and the bones or soft tissue overlying them must be brought together without producing scar tissue or shortening or abnormally thickening the soft palate. The object of surgery is to provide a roof for the mouth and floor for the nose, to ensure that there is adequate movement of the soft palate so that it can effect reasonable closure between the mouth and nose cavities, and also to ensure that there is mobility of the lips without any tightness or constriction. More than one operation may be necessary. A second operation may also be advisable when the soft palate is very mobile, and a large space exists between the soft palate and back of the throat, preventing reasonable closure.

Surgery doesn't automatically correct cleft palate speech once these habits of speech have been established. A child should be referred for speech therapy as soon after the operation as the surgeon advises. The success of treatment is influenced by the anatomical and physiological result of surgical treatment, and the age at which treatment begins. The child's intelligence, personality and environment also play a part. So does the accuracy of the child's hearing and his 'speech sense', and existing habits of speech. Where there is a cleft of the hard palate, treatment may also depend upon the severity of dental anomalies which can distort some speech sounds. The child must learn to move his repaired palate in relation to the rest of his speech muscles, to direct the air stream used for speech through the mouth, and to say vowels and consonants correctly so that these can then be introduced into his speech. Such activities as yawning, sucking, holding air pressure in the mouth, and using a straw for cold drinks can be incorporated into games as a means to help the child's speech. Simple rhymes which ensure that sounds are made alternatively in the mouth and nose can promote mobility of the repaired palate. Here are two such rhymes, with actions –

Ding Dong
Ding Dong
Ring the bell (repeat)

or

Bang – Bang – Bang
I play on my drum etc.

The child with a repaired cleft palate needs a lot of ear training to help him to discriminate between sounds. It is very important that children do not strain to make sounds correctly. Parents can be shown by a speech therapist how best they can help their child carry out his speech practice and exercises. He needs plenty of encouragement and reassurance while he is learning to establish and maintain new habits of voice and articulation. This achievement is not made overnight. As the child progresses he will gain confidence in his newly acquired speech and voice habits.

CLEFT PALATE SPEECH

Although the most common cause of this type of speech is a cleft palate, this is not always the case. In some instances, the soft palate may be sluggish or paralysed as a result of polio, diphtheria or some other severe illness. The air used for speech may escape through the nose. Sometimes as a result of the removal of very enlarged adenoids a type of cleft palate speech occurs. With the enlarged adenoids removed, the space at the back of the throat is now large enough to cause voice and articulation difficulties. There are children with perfectly normal palates who have cleft palate speech. They have learned to speak using the wrong positions of the tongue or made inaccurate judgements about the amount of closure of the space at the back of the throat needed for acceptable speech.

A child with a cleft palate needs specialist assessment. The present standard of surgery is excellent and the child may, after the operation, be referred for speech therapy. In cases where it is not feasible to operate, the child may be referred to a specialist dentist (orthodontist) and the possibility of fitting an appliance considered. A speech appliance, removable for hygienic reasons, is anchored to the teeth or in some cases is fitted into the actual cleft of the hard palate. Temporary appliances can be made as early as four years of age. Designing and fitting these appliances must be carried out by an expert as great skill and judgement is required.

MENTAL HANDICAP

There are many varying degrees of mental handicap. It is essential that a child's condition be diagnosed as soon as possible so that he gets the help he needs.

The public is more aware of the real needs of mentally handicapped children today than ever before. Children who were once neglected and hidden are now catered for in special schools and day centres. The purpose of these schools and centres is to provide an opportunity for the child to develop within his capabilities and take his place in society. Care is taken to ensure that each child is professionally assessed and referred for the special help he needs. Besides mental handicap he may have associated defects such as hearing loss, speech or language difficulty which need assessment.

If your child has been diagnosed as having a degree of mental handicap, he may also have associated speech and language difficulties. He may be delayed in developing language, have faulty articulation, have difficulty in remembering what he hears long enough to be able to reproduce it, or may be only partially able to sort out what he hears.

It is quite likely that he will be referred to a special school which is specifically organised to meet his individual needs. Quite often parents feel reluctant to send a child who is mentally handicapped to a special school as they feel there is a stigma attached to it. Instead they may send the child to a school which is not suitable for him. A child in any school will have difficulty in progressing if he is placed in a class where the intelligence level is much higher than his own. Quite often the mentally handicapped child is forced to keep up with a class that is too advanced for him because his parents feel the child will make better progress if stimulated in a 'good' school. This can be a terrible mistake and can also cause frustration for the parents who feel they are doing their best for the child, yet realise he is not responding to their efforts. The situation is also unfair to teachers who cannot possibly be expected to achieve miracles with one mentally handicapped child in a class of children of a higher intelligence level. Many parents understandably have great difficulty in accepting the fact that their child is mentally handicapped. They need constant encouragement and reassurance as well as counselling and advice. The importance of having a child professionally assessed cannot be overstressed since to help a child effectively it is vital to know and come to accept the situation as it really is. A child cannot be expected to progress if the demands made on his ability are too high. It is more helpful to the child who is mentally handicapped to attend a school where his needs are recognised and met effectively and where he has the opportunity to develop his abilities and 'shine' among children of a similar intelligence level.

Since the mentally handicapped child can have speech and language problems, it is vital that he gets help both at school and at home. He may be receiving help from a speech therapist and from the language curriculum at his school. The first aim is to promote and establish communication. The actual articulation of spoken words is of secondary importance to the development of language. It is vital that close co-operation exists between parents, doctors, teachers, and all those involved with the child. In this way, a plan to promote and establish language development at school can be reinforced at home. Since the child is usually distractible, it is helpful if there is a consistency in the methods used to stimulate and increase his growth of language. This will involve establishing a basic vocabulary essential for him to express his needs and relate socially. The social aspect of language is of paramount importance and special schools direct attention to this area. One school for moderately handicapped children, a majority with speech defects, put on an annual show for parents under expert direction. The audience enjoys it and is usually surprised at the high standard displayed. What may not be apparent to the observer is that the show is geared to enable the children with musical and acting talents to express them, while the younger, most distractible group, are usually given colourful roles involving movement and rhythm.

Rhythm, colour, mime and music can be used very successfully with the mentally handicapped child. Clapping in rhythm to words and music can help the child's concentration and focus attention on words in a constructive way. When choosing rhymes it is wise to choose those in keeping with the child's age and ability. The aims of a language curriculum will vary according to a child's level of speech and language development. To start with the aims could be to stimulate the child to respond orally, to encourage him to observe alertly and to listen. He should be encouraged to improve his eye and hand co-ordination and directional sense, and to foster a desire to communicate shared ideas, and to broaden his vocabulary. Later, situations could be created where ideas can be exchanged, and the child encouraged to improve his auditory and visual discrimination. Formal handwriting could perhaps be introduced. Later still, the aims could be to present patterns of acceptable speech in social situations, encouraging the child to express his ideas and emotions in complete sentences, and perhaps to begin spelling. At a more advanced stage, the aims could be to develop the facility of expressing ideas and perhaps writing.

Associations which help the mentally handicapped child, and encourage and reassure the parents, perform a vital function. As stated earlier, do not settle for second best in terms of the odd few hints picked up at random. Your child needs to be professionally helped and most importantly needs to be helped effectively at home. This means knowing exactly what your child's needs are and how they can be met. It is important to remember, when stimulating a language response from a child with a mental handicap, that he develops language as other children do but at a slower rate. He needs to be stimulated to progress from his present level. If he is only saying 'da' or 'ba', he will need to progress to babbling streams of sound before we can expect him to say words and later speak in sentences. It is also important to realise that the child's span of concentration is apt to be brief. When the child makes an effort to communicate, he needs to be praised. With encouragement and practical help he can be stimulated to use more language more effectively.

DOWN'S SYNDROME

In the past, the 'mongol child', as he used to be called, was often rejected and treated as a burden. Today, parents and doctors who care for these children prefer to call the condition Down's Syndrome. (This syndrome which is characterised by mental retardation, congenital abnormalities and a mongoloid facial appearance was first described by Langdon Down in 1866). Changing the name used to describe the condition is helping to change the stigma which used to be attached to mongolism.

A child with Down's Syndrome is born with an extra chromosome. This condition is nearly always diagnosed at birth. Previously concern was directed towards making allowances for the child whereas now there is a drive towards helping the baby and child achieve his fullest potential. Recent research shows that when a baby with Down's Syndrome is stimulated from birth, his consequent performance seems to indicate the presence of greater ability than at first assumed.

The child can be slow in developing language and poor muscle tone can affect the articulation of speech.

It is possible now for the mother of a Down's Syndrome baby to be visited in hospital by a member of the Down's Syndrome Association before she and the new baby go home. This can be arranged by a hospital social worker. It is usually helpful for parents to share experiences with other parents in a constructive and encouraging atmosphere.

THE APHASIC CHILD

The child who is aphasic can have difficulty in understanding both spoken and written language, and for this reason, the condition is sometimes confused with deafness. The aphasic child may be able to understand language but experience difficulty in expressing his thoughts both verbally and in writing. He can have difficulty in both understanding and expressing language. Neurological assessment is essential. The aphasic child is usually referred for speech therapy which is aimed to suit the needs of that particular child. He can be helped with treatment — progress however, can be slow.

THE AUTISTIC CHILD

Although the specific causes of autism are unknown, treatment is available to alleviate this condition. The autistic child can be withdrawn and experiences great difficulty in expressing himself through language. He can show signs of frustration in his behaviour which can contain disturbances of habit, obsessions, nervous disorders etc. Diagnosis and referral for treatment is necessary. A speech therapist works as a member of a team with psychiatrists, psychologists, doctors and teachers, to help remove the barriers blocking communication.

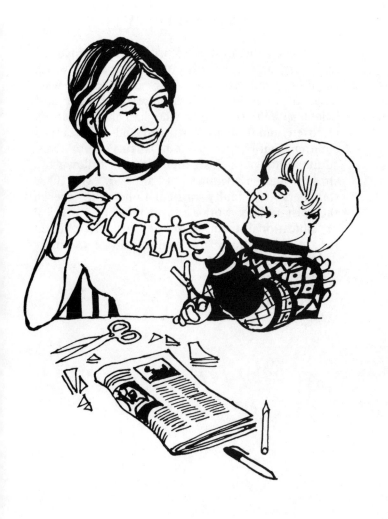

A child needs plenty of encouragement while he is learning new habits of voice and speech.

SPEECH THERAPY

A speech therapist is someone who is qualified to assess and treat disorders of speech, voice, language, and rhythm. This involves a wide range of cases and includes the child with cleft palate speech; the adult who has had his larynx removed; emotionally disturbed and handicapped children with speech and language problems; adults who have lost their speech following a stroke; and individuals of all ages who have stammers or faulty articulation. The speech therapist usually works as a member of a medical or educational team. Cases are usually referred for speech therapy by medical officers, family doctors, and specialists.

Guide To Reference Numbers

1. Sheridan, Mary D., O.B.E., M.A., M.D., D.C.H., F.F.C.M., *The Developmental Progress of Infants and Young Children.* Report 102 Ministry of Health, H.M.S.O. London. 1960. Also: Gesell, Arnold, *The First Five Years of Life,* Methuen 1971.

2. Erikson, Erik H., *Childhood and Society.* Penguin Books 1965.

3. Van Riper, Charles, *Speech Correction Principles and Methods.* Constable & Co. Ltd. 1954.

4. Van Riper, Charles, *Speech Correction Principles and Methods.* Constable & Co. Ltd. 1954.

5. Beadle, Muriel, *A Child's Mind.* Methuen & Co. Ltd., 1971.

6. Thurburn, Gwynneth, *Voice and Speech, An Introduction.* Aberdeen University Press, 1955.

Glossary Of Technical Terms

Articulation — co-ordinated movements of the speech organs.

Audiologist — a specialist in hearing and disorders of hearing.

Chromosome — one of the structures which occur in all living cells and which carry the hereditary factors (genes).

Genetics — a branch of biology concerned with hereditary factors.

Neurological — associated with the nervous system.

Orthodontics — study of the normal formation of the teeth and the correction of malformations.

Psychiatrist — a doctor who is specially qualified in the field of mental health.

Psychologist — someone qualified in the study of psychology, science of the human mind.

Helpful Books

PICTURE BOOKS

Baby's First Book: Ladybird
A.B.C.: Ladybird
Talkabout Series: Ladybird
A.B.C. Word Book, by Richard Scarry: Collins, 1975
Storybook Dictionary: Hamlyn
Beginner's Book Dictionary: Collins
McDonald A.B.C.: McDonald

RHYMES AND JINGLES

This little Puffin, by Matterson: Young Puffin 1969
Puffin Book of Nursery Rhymes, by I. & P. Opie: Puffin 1970
Young Puffin Book of Verse: Penguin
I saw a ship a-sailing, by B. Montresor: Collins
A Golden Land, by James Reeves: Young Puffin 1973
1, 2, 3, 4, by Grace & Wrigley: Warne
Acting Rhymes, Book 1, by E. D. Sanson: Black 1975

ENJOYABLE NON-FICTION BOOKS

Basic Starters Series: McDonald Educational
I can read, by D. Bruna: Methuen
I can read more, by D. Bruna: Methuen
Miffy at the Zoo, by D. Bruna: Methuen
Snow,
The Rabbit, John Burningham: Jonathan Cape
Snow, by John Burningham: Jonathan Cape
School, by John Burningham: Jonathan Cape
The Baby, by John Burningham: Jonathan Cape
What do People Do all Day? by Richard Scarry: Collins 1975
Great Big Schoolhouse, by Richard Scarry: Collins 1975
Books For Me To Begin In, by Ronald Ridout: Purnell

STORY BOOKS

My first Story, by Eileen Colwell: Young Puffins
Tell me a Story (under fives), by E. Colwell: Young Puffins
Tell me Another Story (four to six), by E. Colwell: Young Puffins
Playtime Stories, by Joyce Donoughue: Young Puffins 1974
Jackanory Books: B.B.C. 1974
Colour Knight Series: Hodder
The John Mouse Series, by Roger Hargreaves: Fabri Books
Teeny Tiny Tales: Hamlyn 1970
Storychair Series: Transworld
Picture Lion Series (three to six): Collins
Piccolo Picture Books: Collins
Funniest Story Book Ever, by Richard Scarry: Collins 1975
Dr. Seuss Series: Collins

ACTIVITY BOOKS

Play and Learn Series: Methuen Children's Books Ltd.
3, 4, 5 Basic Learning Books: Kiddicraft
Ladybird Playbooks: Ladybird

GENERAL

The Psychology of Play, by S. Millar: Pelican 1971
The Penguin Book of Playgroups, by Lucas and McKennell: Penguin

Children need to hear speech spoken clearly
and reasonably slowly, and need to be
encouraged to talk in a stimulating and
unhurried atmosphere.

Useful Addresses Ireland

Association for the Welfare of Children in Hospital (Ireland)
51 Mount Prospect Avenue,
Clontarf, Dublin 3.

A.W.C.H. (I) is a voluntary organisation formed to promote the welfare of children in hospital. It is affiliated to N.A.W.C.H. in Britain.

Down's Syndrome Association
St. Michael's House
Goatstown, Dublin 14.

The association works generally in close liaison with geneticists, child psychiatrists and psychologists and urges State and Health boards to provide facilities which could improve the potential development of their children.

Dublin College of Speech Therapy,
129 Merrion Road, Dublin 14.

This college trains students to become speech therapists. It has details of speech therapy services in Ireland.

Dyslexia Association of Ireland,
31 Stillorgan Park
Blackrock, Co. Dublin.

The association is affiliated to the British Dyslexia Association, Bath and helps children of average intelligence who have reading difficulty.

Irish Association of Speech Therapists (I.A.S.T.)
85A Marlborough Road, Dublin 4.

This association has details of Irish speech therapy services and keeps a register of qualified speech therapists.

Irish Pre-School Playgroups Association,
c/o St. Brigid's Nursery,
Mountjoy Square Park, Dublin 1.

The association promotes the formation of playgroups in Ireland for the pre-school child and gives help and advice to organisers.

National Association for Cerebral Palsy (Ireland) Ltd.
St. Brendan's,
Sandymount Ave., Ballsbridge,
Dublin 4.

In residential and outpatient clinics, children with cerebral palsy are assessed and given specialist treatment. There are facilities for small sheltered workshops in Dublin and Cork.

The Association of Parents and Friends of
Mentally Handicapped Children,
St. Michael's House,
Willowfield Park, Goatstown, Dublin 14.

The aims of the association are to help mentally handicapped children and their parents.

The Irish Society for Autistic Children,
32 Merton Rd.,
Rathmines, Dublin 6.

The society has residential and day centres plus sheltered workshops for autistic and emotionally disturbed children and adolescents. It is affiliated to the National Society for Autistic Children and The National Association for the Deaf.

The National Association for the Deaf,
25 Lr. Leeson Street,
Dublin.

The basic function of N.A.D. is to provide for the deaf and hard of hearing in Ireland improved conditions and opportunities relating to diagnosis and treatment — education — employment — accommodation — social life — and advancement in the community.

Britain

AFASIC (Association for all Speech Impaired Children),
Room 14 Toynbee Hall,
28 Commercial Street, London E1 6LS

Afasic is a voluntary association of parents whose children
suffer from speech and language difficulties and of
professionals concerned with these problems. It provides
an advisory service for parents and others.

Association for the Welfare of Children in Hospital,
Exton House,
7 Exton Street, London.

NAWCH is concerned with the welfare of children in
hospital.

British Dyslexia Association,
18, The Circus, Bath.

Children with reading problems are assessed and helped by
this association, which is affiliated to The Dyslexia
Association in Ireland.

Down's Babies Association,
Quinborne Community Centre,
Ridgeacre Road, Birmingham B332TW.

Down's babies are helped by this association, and parents
are given practical advice about treatment methods etc.

National Society for Mentally Handicapped Children,
Pembridge Hall,
17 Pembridge Square, London.

The aims of this Society are to help mentally handicapped children and their parents.

Pre-School Playgroups Association,
Alford House, Aveline Street, London SE11 5DH.

This Association promotes the formation in Britain of pre-school playgroups and advises and helps organisers.

The College of Speech Therapists,
47, St. John's Wood High Street,
London NW8 7NJ.

This college keeps a register of qualified speech therapists and has details of speech therapy services in Britain.

The National Deaf Children's Society,
31, Gloucester Place, London W1H 4EA.

The welfare of the deaf child and help and advice for parents are the aims of this Society.

The National Society for Autistic Children,
1A Golders Green Rd.,
London NW11 8EA.

This Society promotes the mental and physical welfare of autistic and severely disturbed children.

The Spastics Society,
12 Park Crescent, London WIN 4EQ.

A voluntary body which aims to assess and help children with cerebral palsy. Help and advice is given to parents.

U.S.A

American Speech and Hearing Association,
9030 Old Georgetown Rd.,
Washington D.C. 20014, U.S.A.

American Cleft Palate Association,
c/o Gary R. Smiley, D.D.S., M.Sc.,
School of Dentistry,
University of North Carolina,
Chapel Hill, North Carolina 27514, U.S.A.

Association for Children with Learning Disabilities,
2200 Brownsville Rd.,
Pittsburgh, Pennsylvania 15210, U.S.A.

Council for Exceptional Children,
Jefferson Plaza Suite 900,
1499 Jefferson Davis Highway,
Arlington, Virginia 22202, U.S.A.

Information Center for Heating, Speech, and
Disorders of Human Communication,
310 Harriet Lane Home,
John Hopkins Medical Institution,
Baltimore, Maryland 21205, U.S.A.

National Association of the Deaf,
814 Thayer Ave.,
Silver Spring, Maryland 20910, U.S.A.

National Association for Retarded Children,
1522 K St., NW.,
Washington D.C. 20005, U.S.A.

Special Education Information Centre,
1828 L St., N.W., Suite 702,
Washington D.C. 20036, U.S.A.

United Cerebral Palsy Association Inc.,
66 East 34th Street,
New York, New York 10016, U.S.A.

U.S. Department of Health, Education and Welfare,
Bureau of Education for the Handicapped,
Regional Office Building 3, Room 2019,
7 and D Streets, S.W.,
Washington D.C. 20202, U.S.A.

Bibliography

Beadle, Muriel, 1971. *A Child's Mind:* Methuen
Beard, Ruth M., 1972. *An Outline of Piaget's Developmental Psychology:* Routledge & Kegan Paul.
Bowlby, John, 1965. *Child Care & the Growth of Love:* Penguin.
Brown, Roger, 1973. *A First Language The Early Stages:* Allen & Unwin.
Chomsky, Naom, 1968. *Language and Mind:* Harcourt, Brace & World.
Ewing, Sir Alexander & Lady E., 1971. *Hearing Impaired Children: Under Five:* Manchester University Press.
Foss, Brian, Edited by, 1974. *New Perspectives in Child Development:* Penguin.
Gesell, Arnold, 1971. *The First Five Years of Life:* Methuen.
Gollnitz, G., Schulz-Wulf, G., 1973. *Rhythmisch-Psychomotorische Musiktherapie:* Gustav Fischer.
Hahn, Eugene F., 1956. *Stuttering – Significant Theories & Therapies:* Stanford University Press, California.
Lucas and McKennell, 1974. *The Penguin Book of Playgroups:* Penguin.
Matherson, E. M., 1965. *Play with a Purpose for Under Sevens:* Penguin.
Oakeshott, Edna, O.B.E., B.Sc., Ph.D., 1973. *The Child Under Stress:* Priory Press.
Piaget & Inhelder, B., 1969. *The Psychology of the Child:* Routledge & Kegan Paul.
Slobin, D.I., 1971. *Psycholinguisticis:* Scott & Foresman.
Spock, Dr. Benjamin, 1957. *Baby and Child Care:* Pocket Books, New York.
Thurburn, Gwynneth L., 1955. *Voice and Speech – An Introduction:* Aberdeen University Press.
Van Riper, Charles, 1954. *Speech Correction, Principles and Methods:* Constable.
Watts, A. F., D. Lit., (London), 1964. *The Language and Mental Development of Children:* George G. Harrap.
Whetnall E., and Fry, D.B., 1969. *The Deaf Child:* W. Heinemann Medical Books.
Whetnall, E. & Fry, D.B., 1970. *Learning to Hear:* W. Heinemann Medical Books.

Index

157